Faith at the Crossroads

FAITH
AT THE
CROSSROADS
responding to the challenges of life

ROBERT JEFFRESS

BROADMAN PRESS
Nashville, Tennessee

© Copyright 1989 • Broadman Press
All rights reserved
4250-73

0-8054-5073-4
Dewey Decimal Classification: 248.4
Subject Headings: BIBLE - BIOGRAPHY//CHRISTIAN LIFE
Library of Congress Catalog Card Number: 88-38966

Printed in the United States of America

Library of Congress Cataloging-in-Publication Data

Jeffress, Robert, 1955-
    Faith at the crossroads / Robert Jeffress.
        p. cm.
    ISBN 0-8054-5073-4
    1. Bible—Biography. 2. Christian life—1960-   I. Title.
BS571.J44 1989   88-38966
220.9′2—dc19   CIP

Foreword

Faith at the Crossroads! Faith always seems to be at the crossroads. The very image of the word *faith,* called to the computer screen of our mental perception, is that of confrontation with the unknown while trusting the demonstrable faithfulness of our Lord.

Nowhere could one find more stunning portrayal of the exigencies of life, which are characteristic of us all, than in the biographies of biblical people. The stories of patriarchs, matriarchs, apostles, and prophets are not present in the Bible to entertain us but to edify us. How often have you heard someone say, "I really identify with Simon Peter"? To no lesser degree do we find points of poignant identification with a multitude of people presented on the pages of sacred Scripture.

Seldom will be found in the mind of a young man perceptions such as those you are about to read. Dr. Robert Jeffress of the First Baptist Church of Eastland, Texas, has brought years of intense study, remarkable observation of our human dilemmas, and the heart of the pastor to an examination of those crossroads which all of us have either reached or find ourselves approaching. Whether it is the example of Moses being used in his senior years, an image patently and understandably dear to my own soul, or of Ruth remaining faithful despite the cost, Dr. Jeffress has captured the spiritual secrets of the Lord's saints and given us guidance for troubled days.

No chapter is more important than the one on Joseph and bitterness. It alone will be worth the price of the book and the investment of time in reading. God bless the patient pastor for his writing diligence and you, the reader, as you pore over these timely expositions.

W. A. CRISWELL
Pastor's Study
First Baptist Church, Dallas

Preface

Do you remember Robert Frost's poem, "The Road Not Taken"? It tells the story of a traveler who came to a crossroad. He had to decide which road to take. Two roads—two choices.

Faith at the Crossroads tells the story of fifteen men and women who faced familiar crises in their lives—temptation, betrayal, depression, childlessness, and death. Each had to choose how to respond, and each one chose to take the "road less traveled"—the road of faith.

I am indebted to my wife, Amy, for her helpful insights, and to Broadman for encouraging me.

My prayer is that these pages will motivate you in your Christian walk to imitate the lives of these men and women of faith.

Contents

1
Abraham
Answering Yes to the Impossible

One of my family's favorite ways to pass the time while driving on a long trip is playing the game "Who am I?" Remember how the game works? Someone gives a clue, and you try to guess who they have in mind. Let's take a minute and play the game of "Who am I?" based on several Old Testament characters. If I were to say "strength," who would come to mind? Probably Samson. How about "wisdom"? I imagine you are thinking about Solomon. When I say "adultery," who do you think of? I can hear everyone saying in unison, "David!" Let's try one more: "faith." Certainly many Old Testament saints exercised a strong belief in God at a particular juncture in their lives. Yet, one patriarch's life exemplified this character quality for over one hundred years.

When the New Testament writer James was trying to think of someone who represented true faith—the kind of faith that saves—his thoughts turned immediately to Abraham:

> Was not Abraham our father justified by works, when he offered up Isaac his son on the altar? You see that faith was working with his works, and as a result of the works, faith was perfected: and the scripture was fulfilled which says, "And Abraham believed God, and it was reckoned to Him as righteousness," and he was called the friend of God (Jas. 2:21-23).

Why is Abraham the prime example of faith to all Christians? Because of his willingness to say yes when God asked him to do the impossible. In this chapter, we will examine carefully the test Abraham experienced from the hand of God and draw several principles about testing which help you to say yes when God asks you for the ultimate sacrifice.

Preparation for the Test

As we travel with James back in time to Genesis 22, we discover these words, "Now it came about after these things, that God tested Abraham, and said to him, 'Abraham!' And he said, 'Here I am' " (v. 1). Any perceptive Bible student would immediately want to know, "After *what* things?

When Abraham was seventy-five years old, God spoke to him and told him to leave his home in Ur and his relatives for a land that God would show him. Included in that message to Abraham was the promise that he would be the father of a great nation (Gen. 12:1-3). As you can imagine, Abraham had his moments of doubt. How could an elderly man and a barren wife be the nucleus of a nation that would number as the stars of heaven?

After approximately ten years had passed since God's original promise, Abraham began to become nervous. He was eighty-five, and Sarai, seventy-five. The prospects for a large family, or *any* family, were looking grim! So Sarai devised a plan to "help" God fulfill His promise: "So Sarai said to Abram, 'Now behold, the Lord has prevented me from bearing children. Please go in to my maid; perhaps I shall obtain children through her.' And Abram listened to the voice of Sarai" (Gen. 16:2).

Now that idea seems extremely immoral to those of us who are the recipients of the full revelation of God in Scripture. Yet, in Abraham's day this plan did not represent any violation of legal or marital codes. This was the common practice of the day if the wife were unable to conceive. The only problem was that this was not God's plan for fulfilling His promise. In their haste to "assist" God, Abraham and Sarah forgot to talk with God to see if this plan was in keeping with His will.

Abraham was eighty-six years old when Hagar bore him a son named Ishmael. For the next thirteen years, Abraham enjoyed his son, believing that certainly this was the fulfillment of God's promise of a descendant. However, when Abraham was ninety-nine years old, God appeared to him again with this message:

> "As for Sarai your wife, you shall not call her name Sarai, but Sarah shall be her name. And I will bless her, and indeed I will give you a son by her. Then I will bless her, and she shall be a mother of nations;

kings of peoples shall come from her . . . [she] shall bear you a son, and you shall call his name Isaac; and I will establish My covenant with him for an everlasting covenant for his descendants after him" (Gen. 17:15-16; 19).

Abraham was dumbfounded. "Will a child be born to a man one hundred years old? And will Sarah, who is ninety years old, bear a child?" When Sarah got the news, she broke into laughter, probably picturing how funny she and Abraham would look going to the local PTA meetings! Yet, God was faithful in fulfilling His promise: "So Sarah conceived and bore a son to Abraham in his old age, at the appointed time of which God had spoken to him. And Abraham called the name of his son who was born to him, whom Sarah bore to him, Isaac" (Gen. 21:2-3).

Here at last was the "child of promise," the one through whom God would fulfill the pledge He had made with Abram twenty-five years earlier. One can almost hear the sigh of relief from this old man as he planned to spend his last years enjoying the son he had long awaited. The final verses of Genesis 21 paint a picture of the contentment Abraham and his family were experiencing: "Abraham planted a tamarisk tree at Beersheba, and there he called on the name of the Lord, the Everlasting God. And Abraham sojourned in the land of the Philistines for many days" (vv. 33-34).

Abraham spent many mornings under the shade of his tamarisk tree with Sarah, enjoying the "twilight years" of his life and reflecting on the faithfulness of God, not realizing that the greatest test of his life was just around the corner.

The Test

"Now it came about after these things, that God tested Abraham, . . . And He said, 'Take now your son, your only son, whom you love, Isaac, and go to the land of Moriah; and offer him there as a burnt offering on one of the mountains of which I will tell you' " (Gen. 22:1-2). Why would God test Abraham? Had he not already proved himself to God? The great scholar F. B. Meyer wrote this about testings in our lives: "Satan tempts us that he may bring out the evil that is in our hearts; God tries or tests us that He may bring out all the good . . . trials are, therefore, God's vote of confidence in us."[1]

Yet this particular test represented to Abraham the loss of that which was most important to him—his only son, the son God had promised would be the beginning of a great nation, the son who represented the faithfulness of God in spite of tremendous obstacles, the son who brought joy to Abraham and Sarah in their old age. Why would God want to snatch away the life of this boy? To kill this lad would not only result in emotional turmoil for Abraham but also would represent to Abraham the death of God's promise.

Abraham's Response

After receiving such a command, most of us would probably question whether we really had heard the voice of God. Or we might be outraged that God would ask such a thing—but not Abraham. He had heard the voice of God too often during his long life to mistake it for something else. Furthermore, he realized it was perfectly within God's right to request whatever He wished.

No doubt Abraham had witnessed child sacrifices in Mesopotamia, as this was also the practice of the Canaanite religion. These Canaanites, desperate to atone for their sins and to appease their angry gods, would offer their firstborn sons as a propitiation for their transgressions. These fathers did not love their sons any less than others. But their ignorance and superstition, coupled with their awareness of sin, compelled them to extremes.

As Abraham witnessed these sacrifices, he was no doubt grateful that his God had never asked for such a sacrifice. But he was not surprised when the command came. Did Abraham linger after the command to argue with God about this request? No, the Scripture records that "Abraham rose early in the morning and saddled his donkey, and took two of his young men with him and Isaac his son; and he split wood for the burnt offering, and arose and went to the place of which God had told him" (v. 3). Abraham's obedience was immediate: He arose early in the morning and set out toward the place of sacrifice.

The journey to Moriah was about fifty miles and required three days. I imagine that as they walked together Isaac, now a strong and vigorous teenager, made many attempts to talk with his father. But Abraham remained silent as he reflected on God's command and the devastating effect it would have on his life. I am sure Abraham had to ask God for the strength to take every step on the journey to the mountain of sacrifice.

At the end of three days, they saw the mountain from a distance, "and Abraham said to his young men, 'Stay here with the donkey, and I and the lad will go yonder; and we will worship and return to you" (v. 5). At this point we catch a glimpse of Abraham's faith in God. Notice he said to his men, "We will worship and [we] will return to you." Abraham had resolved whatever doubts he had during the journey to Moriah. He was convinced that God was going to be faithful in fulfilling His promises to him. The author of Hebrews wrote this about Abraham:

> By faith Abraham, when he was tested, offered up Isaac; and he who had received the promises was offering up his only begotten son; it was he to whom it was said, "In Isaac your descendants shall be called." He considered that God is able to raise men even from the dead; from which he also received him back as a type (11:17-19).

Even though God's command seemed to contradict His promise, Abraham did not submit to his own limited understanding but kept repeating to himself the truth that God is able!

> Abraham took the wood of the burnt offering and laid it on Isaac his son, and he took in his hand the fire and the knife. So the two of them walked on together. And Isaac spoke to Abraham his father and said, "My father!" And he said, "Here I am, my son." And he said, "Behold, the fire and the wood, but where is the lamb for the burnt offering?" (Gen. 22: 6-7).

As a youth, Isaac often had observed his father offering a lamb as a burnt offering to God. This was a natural question for him to ask. The question was like a knife plunged into Abraham's heart reminding him of the task that lay before him.

Yet Abraham's faith in the goodness and the faithfulness of God remained steadfast: "Abraham said, 'God will provide for Himself the lamb for the burnt offering, my son.' So the two of them walked on together" (v 8). Then came the moment when Abraham had to reveal the full truth to Isaac: "Then they came to the place of which God had told him; and Abraham built the altar on top of the wood" (v. 9). Scripture draws a veil over this most tender moment as Abraham revealed to his son the command of the Lord, as Isaac also willingly submitted to the will of God, and as they embraced one last time.

At this point, one surely becomes aware that this event was a foreshadowing of the submission of God's only Son to a sacrificial death. Jesus, too, carried the wood on His back to the mount of sacrifice—very likely in this same location—and laid Himself on the altar. Like the strong and able Isaac, Jesus Christ could have rebelled and refused the command of His Father, but instead He "emptied Himself, taking the form of a bond-servant, and being made in the likeness of men. And being found in appearance as a man, He humbled Himself by becoming obedient to the point of death, even death on a cross" (Phil. 2:7-8).

I believe that at this moment all activity in heaven ceased, and the angels looked down with wonder and amazement as "Abraham stretched out his hand, and took the knife to slay his son" (v. 10). Was it possible that mortal man loved God so much he was willing to sacrifice what was dearest to him? The Eternal God must have been moved to the very depths of His being as He called out to his faithful servant, "Abraham, Abraham! . . . Do not stretch out your hand against the lad, and do nothing to him; for now I know that you fear God, since you have not withheld your son, your only son, from Me" (Gen. 22: 11-12).

Results of the Test

What was the result of Abraham's obedience to God? First, God provided the sacrifice: "Then Abraham raised his eyes and looked, and behold, behind him a ram caught in the thicket by his horns; and Abraham went and took the ram, and offered him up for a burnt offering in the place of his son. And Abraham called the name of that place The Lord Will Provide, as it is said to this day, 'In the mount of the Lord it will be provided' " (vv. 13-14).

God was teaching not only Abraham but all humanity the most basic spiritual lesson: Human beings are incapable of providing an adequate sacrifice for their sins. "For it is impossible for the blood of bulls and goats to take away sins" (Heb. 10:4). God had to provide the ultimate substitutionary sacrifice for our sins "the Lamb of God who takes away the sin of the world!" (John 1:29). Thus, it was to be in that same mountainous area, two thousand years later, that God "would provide" the Lord Jesus Christ as our sin substitute.

The second result of Abraham's obedience was God's renewed commitment God to fulfill His promise to Abraham. But this time, instead of just promising, God swore His blessing to Abraham. And since there was none greater, God swore by His own name:

> "By Myself I have sworn, declares the Lord, because you have done this thing, and have not withheld your son, your only son, indeed I will greatly bless you, and I will greatly multiply your seed as the stars of the heavens, and as the sand which is on the seashore; and your seed shall possess the gate of their enemies. And in your seed all the nations of the earth shall be blessed, because you have obeyed My voice" (Gen. 22:16-19).

The third result of Abraham's obedience is seen in James 2:23. At this moment Abraham entered into a new relationship with God. Although he had been "justified," or made right with God, because of his faith forty years earlier, Abraham was now called "the friend of God." Can you imagine any greater compliment than to be called "the friend of God"? It was a phrase God would use for all eternity to describe His servant who had truly demonstrated his love for God (see Isa. 41:8; 2 Chron. 20:7).

Truth's About God's Testing

Not only can we derive great theological principles from this account but I believe we also can see three eternal truths about testing in a believer's life.

Sometimes Contradict Reason

The command to sacrifice Isaac seemed illogical. Hadn't God promised Abraham that he would be the father of a great nation? Isaac was the beginning of the fulfillment of that promise! And now, God wanted Isaac to die?

Many times God's commands may seem illogical in light of what has previously been revealed to us. Our perspective is limited. Only God sees the big picture. The eternal wisdom of God should cause us to obey His voice in spite of what seems to be logical. The hymn writer expressed it best:

God holds the key of all unknown, and I am glad:
If other hands should hold the key,
Or if He trusted it to me,
I might be sad.

The very dimness of my sight makes me secure;
For, groping in my misty way,
I feel His hand; I hear Him say,
"My help is sure."

Touch Us in Our Most Tender Areas

How often we say to God, "I'm and willing to give you everything in my life, except _____" Isn't it amazing how quickly God cuts through those "everythings" and goes directly to that one "except"? God is not interested in the trivial. His testing, like that of Abraham, involves those things most important to us.

David recognized this truth when he said, "I will not offer burnt offerings to the Lord my God which cost me nothing" (2 Sam. 24:24). God wants to teach us not to build our lives around our possessions or relationships. Only God is capable of satisfying our deepest desires. Corrie Ten Boom said, "I have learned to hold those things dearest to me loosely in my hand. That way it does not hurt as much when God prys them from my hand."

Are Designed for Our Strengthening

Unlike the temptations of Satan, the tests of God are designed to purify us, to make us stronger. When a craftsman wants to make a piece of gold jewelry from a mold, he first melts a piece of unformed gold to burn off all the impurities. How does he know when this is accomplished? The molten gold is pure when the craftsman can see his reflection in the liquid gold. In the same way, through the scorching heat of trials, Christ burns the impurities out of our lives so that His image can be clearly seen.

God was working out an eternal purpose through Abraham. And, as in the case of any man or woman whom God is going to use significantly, God used many tests to mold Abraham into His instrument. Someone has well said, "It is doubtful that God can use any man greatly, until He has hurt him deeply." Are you ready to be used by God? Before you answer too quickly, picture in your mind that which is most important to you. Then, ask yourself the question Abraham had to answer, "Am I willing to sacrifice that possession, that relationship, or that dream because of my love for God?" God's tests are never easy, yet they are necessary if He is going to use us.

> When God wants to drill a man,
> And thrill a man,
> And skill a man,
> When God wants to mold a man
> To play the noblest part;
> When He yearns with all his heart
> To create so great and bold a man
> That all the world shall be amazed,
> Watch His methods, watch His ways!
> How He ruthlessly perfects
> Whom He royally elects!
> How He manners him and hurts him,
> And with mighty blows converts him
> Into trial shapes of clay which
> Only God understands;
> While his tortured heart is crying
> And he lifts beseeching hands!
> How He bends but never breaks
> When his good He undertakes;
> How He uses whom He chooses,
> And with every purpose fuses him;
> By every act induces him
> To try His splendor out—
> God knows what He's about.[2]

2
Job
Three Secrets for Survival

In his book *Loving God,* Charles Colson told the story of Bill Bontrager—a successful judge who became a Christian. But instead of becoming more successful, Bontrager's Christian convictions cost him his job. Colson closed the story with these words: "Obedience to God does not always mean a happy ending. But, then again, why should we think that it would?"[1]

I'm convinced that we hear too many "happy-ending" stories from Christians. You know the kind—"My business was going down the tubes, my children were running wild in the streets, and my wife was ready to leave me. But then I met Jesus, and now my business is grossing a billion dollars a year, my kids are being interviewed on 'Focus on the Family' next week, and my wife thinks she is married to Tom Selleck. Isn't Jesus wonderful!"

When we bombard people with these kinds of stories, we give them the idea that the call to salvation is an automatic exemption from pain and testing. Nothing could be further from the truth. As we look through the pages of the Bible, we quickly come to the conclusion that suffering is the norm, not the exception, for God's people. That's why James wrote, "Consider it all joy, my brethren, when you encounter various trials" (Jas. 1:2). Notice that James did not say "*If* you encounter various trials," but "when." Testing is inevitable for every Christian.

The testing that God allows in our lives might come from any number of sources. It may come from *circumstances* (sickness, financial ruin, loss of a job). *People* may be the source of our testing. In fact, 1 Peter, which is a survival manual on suffering, lists four potential categories of people who might be the source of conflict: employers or employees, husbands or wives, children or parents, and unbelievers. Also included in that letter are ways to deal with each of those conflicts.

Our own carnal *desires* are a source of testing. Peter wrote, "Beloved, I urge you as aliens and strangers to abstain from fleshly lusts, which wage war against the soul" (1 Pet. 2:11).

Finally, *Satan,* can be a source of testing for the Christian (regardless of what the Church Lady on "Saturday Night Live" says): "Be of sober spirit, be on the alert. Your adversary, the devil, prowls about like a roaring lion, seeking someone to devour" (1 Pet. 5:8).

How can you survive the testing that will come into your life? Studying the life of Job gives some concrete help. In fact, when James wrote about patience and endurance during testing, he singled out Job as an example of a right response to suffering.

Let's first look at the trouble Job experienced.

The Man from Uz

We find a biographical sketch of Job in the opening verses of Job 1. He was a contemporary of Abraham. He possessed great wealth—in fact, he "was the greatest of all the men in the east" (Job 1:3). But the most important word about Job is found in the opening verse of the book: "There was a man in the land of Uz, whose name was Job, and that man was blameless, upright, fearing God, and turning away from evil" (1:1).

The scene shifted from earth to heaven. Satan was in the presence of God, after walking around the earth. God, proud of His servant Job, began to brag on Job: "Have you considered My servant Job? For there is no one like him on the earth, a blameless and upright man, fearing God and turning away from evil" (1:8).

"Of course, he's righteous," Satan argued. "Look at all You have given him—he'd be a fool not to obey You! But if You were to take it all away, I bet he would curse You instead of praising You."

Someone has said that testing is God's vote of confidence in us. God had confidence enough in Job's faith to allow Satan to bring adversity in his life: "Then the Lord said to Satan, 'Behold, all that he has is in your power, only do not put forth your hand on him.' " So Satan departed from the presence of the Lord" (1:12).

I think it would be helpful to say a word about the difference in testing and temptation. God tests, but Satan tempts. What's the difference? Webster defines *tempt* as "to entice to do wrong by promise of pleasure or gain." In other words, the goal of temptation is to make someone fall. And the Bible teaches that God never tempts anyone.

On the other hand, the goal of testing is to make someone stronger. James said, "The testing of your faith produces endurance" (1:3). Trials are like a refiner's fire used to heat gold or silver. At a certain temperature, the dross rises to the top and is scraped off so that the resulting product is purer and stronger. Testing is a way for God to remove the impurities from our lives. The goal is to make us stronger.

When It Rains, It Pours

We find a vivid description of the catastrophic losses Job suffered. Notice how quickly one followed another. The italics are mine.

> Now it happened on the day when his sons and his daughters were eating and drinking wine in their oldest brother's house, that a messenger came to Job and said, "The oxen were plowing and the donkeys feeding beside them, and the Sabeans attacked and took them. They also slew the servants with the edge of the sword, and I alone have escaped to tell you." *While he was still speaking,* another also came and said, "The fire of God fell from heaven and burned up the sheep and the servants and consumed them; and I alone have escaped to tell you." *While he was still speaking,* another also came and said, "The Chaldeans formed three bands and made a raid on the camels and took them and slew the servants with the edge of the sword; and I alone have escaped to tell you." *While he was still speaking,* another also came and said, "Your sons and your daughters were eating and drinking wine in their oldest brother's house, and behold a great wind came from across the wilderness and struck the four corners of the house, and it fell on the young people and they died; and I alone have escaped to tell you" (1:13-19).

The loss of all of one's possessions and children would be enough to make most Christians throw in the towel. But not Job! We find Job's response to these disasters in the closing verses of chapter 1.

> Then Job arose and tore his robe and shaved his head, and he fell to the ground and worshiped. And he said,/"Naked I came from my mother's womb,/And naked I shall return there./The Lord gave and the Lord has taken away./Blessed be the name of the Lord."/Through all this Job did not sin nor did he blame God (vv. 20-22).

If at First You Don't Succeed . . .

Satan was not through with Job. Again he approached God, arguing that if Job's health were taken away he would turn from God. Still confident in Job's integrity, He gave Satan permission to attack Job; however, Satan could not take Job's life. "Then Satan went out from the presence of the Lord, and smote Job with sore boils from the sole of his foot to the crown of his head. And he took a potsherd to scrape himself while he was sitting among the ashes" (2:7-8).

The Old Testament scholar Meredith Kline wrote this about the nature of Job's illness:

> Modern medical opinion is not unanimous in its diagnosis of Job's disease. But according to the prognosis in Job's day, it was apparently hopeless. The horrible symptoms included inflamed eruptions accompanied by intense itching (2:7-8), maggots in ulcers (7:5), erosion of the bones (30:17), blackening and falling of skin (30:30), and terrifying nightmares (7:14), though some of these may possibly be attributed to the prolonged exposure that followed the onset of the disease. Job's whole body, it seems, was rapidly smitten with the loathsome, painful symptoms. Though Satan had been obliged to spare his victim's life, the sufferer probably thought his death was imminent.[2]

As Job was scraping his boils off with a broken piece of pottery and surrounded by the ruins of his possessions, his wife approached him and said, "Do you still hold fast your integrity? Curse God and die!" (2:9).

But Job's response was, " 'You speak as one of the foolish women speaks. Shall we indeed accept good from God and not accept adversity?' In all this, Job did not sin with his lips" (2:10).

What gave Job the ability to stand firmly in his faith, unswayed by the circumstances? As I look at the life of Job, I find three "secrets" that kept him strong in spite of adversity.

He Refused to Listen to the Ungodly Counsel of Others.

Isn't it amazing how many people have advice to offer when we are suffering? Job had his share of unsolicited counsel. First, he heard from his wife. By all indications she was an unbeliever, therefore, we would not expect her to give godly advice. Her perspective on suffering was like most unbelievers: "If there really were a God, He would deliver you."

Job dismissed this line of reasoning. He realized that adversity is just as much a part of God's plan for His children as is blessing. Furthermore, although he valued his possessions, his children, and his health, he realized that they were "on loan" to him from God.

The advice of his three "friends" was more insidious than his wife's. Space prevents us from looking at each of these men's words to Job. But the sum of what they said was this: "Job, you must have some unconfessed sin in your life that has caused God to punish you. Otherwise, why would you be suffering? For we know that God prospers the godly and punishes evildoers."

It's funny how that same line of reasoning is just as popular today as it was in Job's time. I think the biggest heresy in evangelical Christianity is this prosperity gospel: "God wants every Christian healthy and wealthy." While that sounds good, the corollary of that is lethal: "If you are not prospering and/or you are sick, there is something wrong with your spiritual life."

I know many people who are filled with guilt and feelings of spiritual impotence because of some adversity that has entered their lives. They reason, *If I would believe just a little more, maybe God would remove this problem.*

Let's start telling people the truth. God's plan for Christians does not necessarily include prosperity and health. If it does, Jesus Christ certainly missed out on God's blessings. He wandered about Israel without any possessions and no home and ended up being crucified.

Or think about the apostle Paul. During most of his ministry, he was penniless or in prison. He suffered a physical handicap that God refused to heal. The conclusion of Paul's ministry was less than spectacular—he was beheaded in some obscure prison outside of Rome.

Or consider the first-century Christians: "They were stoned, they were sawn in two, they were tempted, they were put to death with the sword; they went about in sheepskins, in goatskins, being destitute, afflicted, ill-treated" (Heb. 11:37).

If we are going to stand firm in times of testing, we have to reject ungodly advice, whether it comes from unbelievers or from well-meaning, but unwise, friends.

Helping Those Who Hurt

Let me switch perspectives for a moment and give some practical ways that you can be of genuine help to those who are experiencing a great loss. These are ways of helping those who hurt:

Act Genuine

People are always worried about saying the wrong thing to someone who is grieving. But the hurting person will appreciate your honesty. If you were stunned at the news of their loss, say so. If you feel like crying, cry. If you want to hug them and say nothing, do that.

Be Quiet

Ecclesiastes 3:7 says that there is a time to be silent and a time to speak. Don't worry about what to say. Sometimes the best thing to say is nothing. In his book *The Last Thing We Talk About,* Joe Bayley relates an experience after one of his children had died:

> I was sitting, torn by grief. Someone came and talked to me of God's dealings, of why it happened, of hope beyond the grave. He talked constantly, he said things I knew were true.
> I was unmoved, except to wish he'd go away. He finally did.
> Another came and sat beside me. He didn't talk. He didn't ask leading questions. He just sat beside me for an hour and more, listened when I said something, answered briefly, prayed simply, left.
> I was moved. I was comforted. I hated to see him go.[3]

Comfort by Being Supportive

Remember, it's *you* that the grieving person needs, not your words. Haddon Robinson told the story about a little girl whose favorite playmate had died. One day the girl told her parents that she had comforted the grieving mother. "What did you say to her?" the father asked. "Nothing," she replied, "I just climbed up on her lap and cried with her." That's what it means to be supportive.

Do Something Practical

Sometimes the best thing you can do for a grieving person is the dishes! Don't ask, "Is there something I can do?" Just do it! Mowing the lawn, bringing dinner, and picking up the laundry are some practical things that will be of genuine help to someone in sorrow.

He Was Obedient to God in Spite of the Circumstances

Notice that Job still worshiped God when everything was bleak (1:22; 2:10). Though there seemed to be no evidence of God's love and power, he still was obedient. The result was that Job was strengthened. We believe that faith produces obedience, and it does. Right belief produces right actions.

But the opposite is also true. Obedience produces faith. Do the right thing, and you will feel the right thing. There is an inseparable link between faith and obedience. The German pastor Dietrich Bonhoeffer, who was murdered in a Nazi concentration camp, said, "Only he who believes is obedient, only he who is obedient believes."

God is calling you to be obedient in spite of your circumstances. You might be in a difficult marriage and contemplating divorce; you might be suffering a financial disaster and considering a dishonest deal; or, you might be facing a serious illness and be tempted to blame God.

God's message to you is the same as His message to Job: "Obey, even though you can't see the immediate result of your faith."

He Trusted in God's Sovereignty and Goodness

Sure, Job had moments, like all of us, when he wondered if God were in control. But in the end, he expressed his belief in God's sovereignty: "I know that you can do anything and that no one can stop you. You ask who it is who was so foolishly denied your providence. It is I. I was talking about things I knew nothing about and did not understand, things far too wonderful for me" (42:2-3, TLB).

Not only did Job believe in the sovereignty of God but he also was convinced of the goodness of God. That belief gave Job the courage to say, "Though He slay me, I will hope in Him" (13:15).

While God's goodness might not have meant the removal of his present problems, Job believed that it would result in his eternal good. "And as for me, I know that my Redeemer lives,/And at the last He will take His stand on the earth./Even after my skin is destroyed,/Yet from my flesh I shall see God" (19:25-26).

The problem with most of us is that we have a distorted view of the goodness of God. C. S. Lewis put it this way:

> We want, in fact, not so much a Father in Heaven as a grandfather in Heaven . . . whose plan for the universe was simply that it might be truly said at the end of each day, "a good time was had by all." . . . I should very much like to live in a universe which was governed on such lines. But since it is abundantly clear that I don't, and since I have reason to believe, nevertheless, that God is Love, I conclude that my conception of love needs correction . . . . The problem of reconciling human suffering with the existence of a God who loves, is only insoluble so long as we attach a trivial meaning to the word "love".[4]

"Why Me, Lord?"

The Bible doesn't paint Job as a saint. This story is filled with instances in which Job questioned the wisdom and the love of God. You, too, will find yourself wondering why God allows suffering in your life.

As I write these words, I have just finished counseling with a mother who found out her grade-school daughter was molested by an older boy in the neighborhood. The mother kept crying, "Why did you let this happen, Lord? Why?"

Let me share with you what I said to her.

One reason, and the most basic reason, we suffer is because of sin. We live in a fallen world, with fallen people. God's plan for us never included pain, sickness, broken relationships, or even death. All of that is a result of sin. That is why Paul wrote, "We ourselves groan within ourselves, waiting eagerly for our adoption as sons, the redemption of our body" (Rom. 8:23). Christ's return to earth is the only hope we have of having sin's stranglehold on our world broken.

Second, God uses trials to fix our hope on heaven. God doesn't want us to build our lives around possessions or people. Instead, He wants us to be looking forward to heaven. I believe that the more we suffer here, the more we will enjoy heaven. It's like my mother-in-law observed when she was on a diet: "It's odd, but the hungrier you are, the better your food tastes!"

When I was growing up, I used to hear my pastor say, "When I was a youngster, heaven meant very little to me. It was way off there, somewhere, and had little relation to my life. Now that I am an old man, and most of my loved ones are in heaven, it has taken on a new meaning and blessedness to me."

I understood that truth intellectually. But I didn't really understand it until I began to bury friends and family members. Maybe that is what Jesus had in mind when He said, "Where your treasure is, there will your heart be also" (Matt. 6:21).

Third, God allows us to experience certain trials so that we can comfort other Christians when they encounter similar difficulties. If you really take seriously your role as a priest—one who represents God to other people—you will see the truth of this principle as expressed in 2 Corinthians 1:3-4: "Blessed be the God and Father of our Lord Jesus Christ, the Father of mercies and God of all comfort; who comforts us in all our affliction so that we may be able to comfort those who are in any affliction with the comfort with which we ourselves are comforted by God."

In the early days of my ministry, I had to minister to many families who had lost loved ones. Because I had never experienced the death of a loved one, there was an impenetrable barrier between me and the ones I ministered to. But after going through the entire process of a terminal illness and the subsequent death of my mother, I was better able to empathize with those who experienced a similar loss. And more importantly, I was able to share how God ministered to me during the grieving process. I can now honestly thank God for that experience.

Finally, God uses suffering in our lives to make us more like Christ. Do you know what God's will for your life is? It's clearly stated in Romans 8:29: "to become conformed to the image of His Son." God wants to make you just like Jesus. And every circumstance that God allows in your life is designed for that purpose.

How are we made like Christ? It's not through the easy times; it is through the hard circumstances. To me, one of the most amazing verses in the Bible is Hebrews 5:8. Speaking of Christ, the Bible says, "He learned obedience from the things which He suffered." I know that Jesus was totally perfect because He was the unique Son of God. Yet this verse teaches that there was something profitable about His suffering in relationship to His character. And God still uses suffering to develop our characters. That's what prompted Peter to write:

Beloved, do not be surprised at the fiery ordeal among you, which comes upon you for your testing, as though some strange thing were happening to you; but to the degree that you share the sufferings of Christ, keep on rejoicing; so that also at the revelation of His glory, you may rejoice with exultation (Pet. 4:12-13).

Too bad Job didn't have Peter for one of his friends, isn't it?

3
Joseph
Refusing To Let Bitterness Eat Your Lunch

Four American soldiers during the Korean War hired a young national to do their cooking. They thought they would have some fun by playing all sorts of practical jokes on him. For example, while he was asleep at night, they would nail his shoes to the floor; he would arise in the morning, pull the nails out, and never say a word. Or, they would put a bucket of water on top of the door so he would be deluged with water when he opened the door—but again, no word of complaint. Sometimes, they would put grease on the stove handles, but he would simply wipe them off, always keeping a cheery attitude.

The soldiers were ashamed of themselves, especially in light of the boy's good attitude. So they called him in one day to give him the good news.

"We wanted to tell you that we are going to stop playing those tricks on you. Your good attitude has made us feel a little ashamed of ourselves."

The boy's eyes lit up. "You mean, no more nail shoes to floor?"

"That's right."

"You mean, no more water on top of door?"

"We promise."

"And no more grease on stove handles?"

"You have our word."

"All right, then, no more spit in soup!"

How do you respond when you are mistreated? Think for a moment of someone who has wronged you in the last month. It's amazing how quickly we can think of someone, isn't it? It may be a family member who has wronged you, a friend who has betrayed you, or, maybe a business associate who has cheated you out of some money. How do you handle that resentment? Do you find yourself smiling on the outside, while secretly spitting in the soup?

I am convinced that one of the most important decisions a person can make in life is how to respond to mistreatment. You can choose to become bitter, or you can choose to forgive. In this chapter, we are going to look at a man who had every reason to feel bitter, but he resisted the trap of resentment. And his choice to do so had eternal consequences. His name? Joseph.

Scene One: Dothan

Joseph was one of the twelve sons of Jacob. In fact, he was Jacob's favorite, as evidenced by the famous multicolored coat Jacob gave to Joseph. Understandably, the brothers weren't crazy about Joseph. One day Jacob sent Joseph out to check on his brothers, who were tending the sheep. When Joseph finally found them in Dothan, he did not receive a cordial welcome. They wanted to kill him but compromised by selling him into slavery. After dipping Joseph's coat in animal blood, the brothers returned it to their father with the story that a wild animal had killed his favorite son. The Bible says that, upon hearing the news, Jacob mourned the loss of his son for many days (Gen. 37:24).

Scene Two: Meanwhile in Egypt

Through a series of miraculous circumstances, Joseph ended up in Egypt. Pharaoh had some bad dreams. At first, he discounted their importance. *I'll just give up late-night snacking,* he might have resolved. But then he began to worry—maybe those dreams had meanings. Joseph interpreted the dreams for him. Joseph predicted that there would be seven years of plentiful harvest in Egypt, to be followed by seven years of famine that would affect Egypt and all the surrounding land. In response to that vision, Pharaoh gave Joseph a position of authority. Joseph ordered the stockpiling of food during the seven years of abundance.

Scene Three: Back in Canaan

Just as Joseph had predicted, the seven years of famine came to Egypt and to Canaan, where Jacob and his remaining eleven sons lived. When Jacob heard there was food in Egypt, he dispatched his sons to request assistance. Little did they know that the man to whom they would make their request would be their own brother, Joseph.

The Climax

Genesis 45 records the revelation of Joseph to his brothers:

> Then Joseph could not control himself before all those who stood by him, and he cried, "Have everyone go out from me." So there was no man with him when Joseph made himself known to his brothers. And he wept so loudly that the Egyptians heard it, and the household of Pharaoh heard it. Then Joseph said to his brothers, "I am Joseph! Is my father still alive?" But his brothers could not answer him, for they were dismayed at his presence. Then Joseph said to his brothers, "Please come closer to me." And they came closer (vv. 1-4).

They were thinking to themselves, *This is it! Joseph is going to get even with us now!* With sweat pouring down their faces, they moved closer to their brother. But he surprised them with his words:

> "I am your brother Joseph, whom you sold into Egypt. And now do not be grieved or angry with yourselves, because you sold me here; for God sent me before you to preserve life . . . . And God sent me before you to preserve for you a remnant in the earth, and to keep you alive by a great deliverance. Now, therefore, it was not you who sent me here, but God. . . . Hurry and go up to my father, and say to him, "Thus says your son Joseph, "God has made me lord of all Egypt; come down to me, do not delay' " (Gen. 45:4-9).

Following Joseph's instructions, Jacob and his sons went to live in Egypt. At the invitation of Pharaoh, they settled in the fertile region of Goshen. For seventeen years they enjoyed living there. Finally, at the age of 147, Jacob died.

The brothers began to worry. Could Joseph's benevolence and forgiving spirit have been only out of deference to Jacob? Now that Jacob was gone, was Joseph going to seek revenge? The brothers quickly decided to butter up Joseph. "Then his brothers also came and fell down before him and said, 'Behold, we are your servants' " (Gen. 50:18).

But Joseph saw right through them. Sensing the fear in their hearts, he gave them these words of reassurance.

But Joseph said to them, "Do not be afraid, for am I in God's place? And as for you, you meant evil against me, but God meant it for good in order to bring about this present result, to preserve many people alive. So therefore, do not be afraid, I will provide for you and your little ones." So he comforted them and spoke kindly to them (Gen. 50:19-21).

How could Joseph be so gracious to those who had betrayed him? As I look at Joseph, I see four principles that kept Joseph—and will also keep you—from being overtaken by bitterness. When you are mistreated . . .

Never Focus on the Offender's Motivations for Hurting You.

When someone wrongs you, it is natural to ask: Why did he want to do that? or, What does he have against me? or, What's wrong with me that he would want to treat me that way? But if we are not careful, those thoughts will soon become an obsession with us.

Several years ago, a man in one of the churches I served felt like he had been betrayed by a friend. Day after day, he sat in his office stewing over his friend's supposed offense for hours at a time. He started to lose touch with reality. His other friends noticed a radical change in his behavior, and they started to drift away. When I urged him to forgive the person, he responded, "I just can't let go of it." Bitterness can destroy a person's life. And one way to avoid it is by refusing to dwell on the offender's reason for hurting us.

Joseph is a good example for us to follow. He did not sit around Pharaoh's court day and night, sulking and lamenting, "Why did my brothers do this to me?" Make no mistake about it: Joseph recognized the sin of his brothers. He was not some Pollyanna who said, "Now guys, I know you didn't mean to sell me into slavery. You must have been having a bad day. Let's pretend it never happened." No, in Genesis 50:20 he was very blunt: "You meant evil against me." Joseph recognized their sin, but he didn't focus on it. Why?

Joseph believed that his God was bigger than his brothers' actions. His view was like that of the psalmist: "For the wrath of man shall praise Three" (Ps. 76:10). In other words, God can take people's wrong attitudes and actions and use them for His purpose.

David recognized this truth in his life. Do you remember the story in 1 Samuel 26 when he had the opportunity to kill King Saul—the evil monarch who was trying to take David's life? His response to his men was classic: "Do not destroy him, for who can stretch out his hand against the Lord's anointed and be without guilt?" (v. 9).

Can't you hear the objections of David's men? "Saul, God's anointed? You've got to be kidding. He's trying to kill you!"

But David believed in God who was bigger than Saul—a God who could use Saul and all of his evil actions to accomplish His purpose in David's life. Don't miss the point. The reason we are not to focus on the motivations of those who hurt us is because our offenders are under God's control. The writer of Proverbs affirmed: "The king's heart is like channels/of water in the hand of the Lord;/He turns it wherever He wishes (Prov. 21:1).

That truth should be a tremendous source of encouragement for all of us. Husbands and wives, it means that the heart of your spouse—Christian or non-Christian—is in the hand of the Lord. It means that God can work through and in spite of what your spouse might do. Teenagers and parents, it means that your hearts are in God's hands. He can take the wrongs you commit against one another and use them to your benefit. Men and women, it means the heart of your employer is in God's hands. When you are mistreated, God is still on the throne and is working out His plan for your life. That is why we should not become obsessed with trying to figure out why someone has hurt us. That's not the issue. Instead, we should . . .

Focus on God's Eternal Purpose

Joseph focused on God's eternal purpose. Notice how he completed his statement in Genesis 50:20: "And as for you, you meant evil against me, but God meant it for good in order to bring about this present result, to preserve many people alive." Joseph saw the overriding purpose of God in the offense of his brothers. Although his brothers had only evil in their hearts, God was working through them! Think of how God used the brothers' treacherous act. Joseph ended up in Egypt where he became second in command to Pharaoh. And in that position, he was able to provide food for his brothers and father during the famine.

But the good did not stop there. The lives of innumerable Egyptions were saved. Not only were the lives of the immediate family saved, but the in-laws' and children's lives were saved as well—about seventy people. But the good did not stop there! Those seventy people formed the nucleus of the entire nation of Israel. At Pharaoh's invitation, they settled in a prosperous region, and for four hundred years they multiplied into an invincible nation. But the good did not stop there. That nation of several million was led out of Egypt under Moses' direction and eventually settled in the Promised Land. And from that nation the Savior of the world was born.

Think of it! Those good results were accomplished because of an offense toward one man. Had Joseph become bitter against his family, failing to see the providence of God in the situation, he could have refused his brothers' request and allowed them to starve to death. The nation of Israel would never have started, and the promise of a Savior would have been unfulfilled. And you and I would have been left to suffer the consequences of our sins.

The fact that God can use temporary injustices to serve eternal purposes is perfectly illustrated in Acts 2:23-24. Peter was preaching at Pentecost. He was speaking to the same group of Jews that had crucified Christ just a few weeks earlier:

> "Men of Israel, listen to these words: Jesus the Nazarene, a man attested to you by God with miracles and wonders and signs which God performed through Him in your midst, just as you yourselves know— this Man, delivered up by the predetermined plan and foreknowledge of God, you nailed to a cross by the hands of godless men and put Him to death."

Notice the perfect balance between human responsibility and the sovereignty of God. Peter declared that his listeners were responsible for nailing Christ to the cross ("you nailed to a cross by the hands of godless men"). But when they killed Jesus, did God throw up His hands in despair and say, "Oh, no! Look what they've done to my Son!" No, this evil act was all according to God's predetermined plan. They meant it for evil, but God used it for good. Jesus had taught His disciples "that He must go to Jerusalem, and suffer many things from the elders and chief priests and scribes, and be killed, and be raised up on the third day" (Matt. 16:21).

Yes, God was bigger than the Jews or the Romans. He was able to accomplish His purpose of worldwide redemption through their injustice. Did Jesus become bitter at His mistreatment? Remember His response on the cross? "Father, forgive them; for they do not know what they are doing." (Luke 23:34). But I imagine He thought to Himself, *But You know what You are doing through them.* That's how to escape the trap of bitterness! Not by asking what are people doing, but what is God doing—believing that He is capable of using the offenses of others in our lives to bring about His will.

I suppose that, outside of John 3:16, the most-quoted verse in the New Testament is Romans 8:28. You've probably hung onto that verse during some rough spots in your life. The King James Version translates it: "We know that all things work together for good to them that love God, to them who are the called according to his purpose."

Some have interpreted the verse to mean: In every bad thing that happens there must be some good, and the way to keep from becoming bitter is to try and find that good. Unfortunately, that reasoning can sometimes border on the absurd.

When I was growing up, my parents quoted Romans 8:28 all the time when something bad would happen. My brother, sister, and I would be challenged to try and find some good in every hardship. For example, my father worked for the airlines, and as a result, we had the opportunity to travel on free airline passes. The problem was that we could be bumped off of our flight if the plane filled up with paying customers. On many occasions, we found ourselves spending the night in the airport. My parents would say, "Look on the bright side— maybe if we had been on that plane, it would have crashed, and we all would have died!" (I wondered sometimes about those unfortunate passengers who had boarded!).

While I appreciate what my parents were trying to do, that is not what Romans 8:28 is all about. There is not something good in every circumstance. There is not a silver lining in every cloud. The *New American Standard Bible* translates Romans 8:28 more accurately: "We know that God causes all things to work together for good to those who love God, to those who are called according to His purpose."

See the difference? There may be no redeeming value in an isolated circumstance. But the message of Romans 8:28 is that God is powerful enough to take something evil (such as another person's offense) and use it for good. We may or may not be able to see the resulting good. That's why it is important for us to be able to . . .

Separate Our Faith from Our Circumstances.

I was listening to a group of people talk about an individual who was very wealthy. Someone admiringly commented, "He's so laid back!" Another person in the group quickly retorted, "I could be pretty laid back, too, if I had all of his money!"

We all tend to think in those terms. "If only . . .

—my spouse were more ____, I could be a better mate."

—my children were less ____, I could be a better parent."

—my boss would quit ____, I would be a better employee."

—my pastor would start ____, I would be more faithful to my church."

—(person's name) would ____, I could forgive him or her."

The secret to a consistent Christian life is learning to separate our obedience from our circumstances. Biblical faith is believing in God enough to obey, even when we can't see the result of our obedience. That's the single theme of the "faith chapter," Hebrews 11. It speaks of men and women who obeyed God, even though they could not see the full result of their obedience. And that still seems to be God's way of dealing with His children. Chuck Colson made that point in his book *Loving God:*

> In more recent times, the great colonial pastor Cotton Mather prayed for revival several hours each day for twenty years; the Great Awakening began the year he died. The British Empire finally abolished slavery as the Christian parliamentarian and abolitionist William Wilberforce lay on his deathbed, exhausted from his nearly fifty-year campaign against the practice of human bondage. Few were the converts during Hudson Taylor's lifelong mission work in the Orient; but today millions of Chinese embrace the faith he so patiently planted and tended.[1]

Why does God not always allow us to see the result of our obedience? Colson concluded: "Knowing how susceptible we are to success's siren call, God does not allow us to see, and therefore glory in, what is done through us. The very nature of the obedience He demands is that it be given without regard to circumstances or results."[2]

You may wonder what all of this had to do with Joseph. The point is that Joseph did not base his right responses on his circumstances. If he had, he would have become bitter early in his life. Just look at the mistreatment he suffered at the hands of others.

—At seventeen, he was sold into slavery by his brothers.

—Later, he was falsely accused of raping his boss's wife.

—While in prison, he helped two friends get out. Once they were out, they forgot about Joseph.

In today's world of psychoanalysis, no one would expect Joseph to be anything but hostile, given his history! But through every test, Joseph's faith remained steadfast in God. How? It was through his
. . .

Understanding Who God Is

Joseph had a correct understanding of God, a comprehension of God that kept him from despair when adversity struck. This knowledge of the nature of God is demonstrated by Joseph's initial speech to his brothers (the emphasis is mine):

> "Now do not be grieved or angry with yourselves, because you sold me here; *for God* sent me before you to preserve life . . . . *And God* sent me before you to preserve for you a remnant in the earth . . . . Now, therefore, it was not you who sent me here, *but God,*" (Gen. 45: 5, 7, 8).

The Hebrew name Joseph used for God in this passage is *Elohim,* "the God of the universe." Joseph strongly believed in the power and the sovereignty of God. God's will could not be circumvented by the whims of men; He was in control.

Do you believe that? Are you convinced that, in spite of what people do and regardless of what happens, God is still sovereign? I believe that such a conviction is the key to preventing other people and circumstances from mowing you down!

I find this principle illustrated in Genesis 31:2. Jacob, Joseph's father, had worked for his uncle for twenty years. It had been a volatile relationship. However, Jacob had become comfortable living with his uncle, Laban, and tending his flocks. But God had a different plan for Jacob. It was time for him to move back to Canaan. How did God communicate to Jacob that it was time to move? "Jacob saw the attitude of Laban, and behold, it was not friendly toward him as formerly."

Did Jacob become bitter over Laban's sudden change of attitude

toward him? No, he saw the hand of God working through Laban.
Notice what Jacob said to his wives:

> "I see your father's attitude, that it is not friendly toward me as
> formerly, but the God of my father has been with me. And you know
> that I have served your father with all my strength. Yet your father has
> cheated me and changed my wages ten times; however, God did not
> allow him to hurt me" (Gen. 31:5-7).

Jacob's faith was not in Laban, but in God, who was capable of
accomplishing His purpose through Laban. And it was that faith that
kept Jacob from being paralyzed with bitterness. Regardless of Laban's motives (which were very suspect), God was still working.

I've seen that truth in my own life. For a number of years, I had
a happy and productive ministry as an associate in a large church.
Although I had felt the call of God to be a pastor, I had become
comfortable in my associate's role. But God had a different plan for
me—He was ready to move me. How did He get the message to me?
Through a changed attitude in one of my co-workers at the church.
Without cause, this person became hostile toward me and my work.
Amid this conflict, another church asked me to come as their pastor.
I'll have to admit that this hostility from someone who had been a
good friend was a major motivation in my moving to this new place
of service.

Guess what happened? Two weeks after I moved to my new church,
that former co-worker was fired from his position. Had I stayed just
a little longer, my "thorn in the flesh" would have been removed, and
I probably would be there today. But that was not God's plan for my
life. He worked through the wrong actions of another to accomplish
His will.

You may be at a crossroads in your emotional life. You can choose
to forgive that person who has offended you, believing that God will
work through that wrong.

4

Moses
Making It Through Mid-Life Crisis

Life begins at forty. Sure. And Santa Claus is coming to town. Let's face it. Middle age is not all it's cracked up to be. Receding hairlines, drooping stomachs, unrealized dreams, and the realization that time is quickly running out make the "noon" of life (as psychologist Carl Jung called it) a traumatic time for many people.

Jack Benny made millions of Americans laugh by keeping his age at thirty-nine. We laughed because we understood the desire to escape from the grim reality of a life more than half spent.

But I think the most disturbing thought about mid-life is the fear that our opportunity to achieve is almost over. Our culture celebrates the accomplishments of youth. Magazines are full of stories of those who have achieved greatness before their thirtieth birthday. And the implication, though never verbalized, is deafening: If you haven't made it by age __, you never will.

I came across this ad that originally appeared in the *Wall Street Journal* for United Technologies. It exposes the myth that a person is either too old or too young to accomplish certain goals:

IT'S WHAT YOU DO—NOT WHEN YOU DO IT
Ted Williams, at age 42, slammed a home run in his last official time at bat.
Mickey Mantle, age 20, hit 23 home runs his first full year in the major leagues.
Golda Meir was 71 when she became Prime Minister of Israel.
William Pitt II was 24 when he became Prime Minister of Great Britain.
George Bernard Shaw was 94 when one of his plays was first produced.
Mozart was just seven when his first composition was published.
Now, how about this? *Benjamin Franklin* was a newspaper columnist

at age 16 and a framer of the United States Constitution when he was 81.

You're never too young or too old if you've got talent. Let's recognize that age has little to do with ability.[1]

I can think of a man who thought life was over at forty. God, it seemed, had put him on the shelf. All he had to be proud of were past accomplishments. His name? Moses.

Now when we think about Moses, we think about the mighty leader of Israel who stood before Pharaoh, pronouncing the ten plagues upon Egypt. Images of the Exodus, the parting of the Red Sea, and Charlton Heston come to mind. That's Moses. He experienced one success after another. Right? Wrong! An examination of Moses' life reveals that his greatest victories occurred *after age eighty.* And they came only because he had successfully navigated through the storm of a mid-life crisis.

From the Palace to the Prairie

The first forty years of Moses' life are compressed into ten short verses in Exodus. To escape the persecution of Pharaoh against the newborn males of Israel, Moses' mother placed him in a wicker basket that floated on the Nile. Notice the providence of God in what happened to Moses:

> Then the daughter of Pharaoh came down to bathe at the Nile, with her maidens walking alongside the Nile; and she saw the basket among the reeds and sent her maid, and she brought it to her. When she opened it, she saw the child, and behold, the boy was crying. And she had pity on him and said, "This is one of the Hebrews' children." Then his sister said to Pharaoh's daughter, "Shall I go and call a nurse for you from the Hebrew women, that she may nurse the child for you?" And Pharaoh's daughter said to her, "Go ahead." So the girl went and called the child's mother . . . And the child grew, and she brought him to Pharaoh's daughter, and he became her son. And she named him Moses, and said, "Because I drew him out of the water" (2:5-10).

The only other clue we have about Moses' first forty years is found in Acts 7:21-22: "After he had been exposed, Pharaoh's daughter took him away, and nurtured him as her own son. And Moses was educated in all the learning of the Egyptians, and he was a man of power in words and deeds." He was on his way to the top!

But at age forty, Moses' life took an unexpected turn. In an instant, he made a wrong decision that affected his life for the next forty years:

> Now it came about in those days, when Moses had grown up, that he went out to his brethren and looked on their hard labors; and he saw an Egyptian beating a Hebrew, one of his brethren. So he looked this way and that, and when he saw there was no one around, he struck down the Egyptian and hid him in the sand. And he went out the next day, and behold, two Hebrews were fighting with each other; and he said to the offender, "Why are you striking your companion?" But he said, "Who made you a prince or a judge over us? Are you intending to kill me, as you killed the Egyptian?" Then Moses was afraid, and said, "Surely the matter has become known." When Pharaoh heard of this matter, he tried to kill Moses. But Moses fled from the presence of Pharaoh and settled in the land of Midian; and he sat down by a well (Ex. 2: 11-15).

In an instant, Moses had let his temper master him, and he lost everything. He had to flee the court of Pharaoh. No longer was he a possible successor to the ruler of Egypt; he was a fugitive.

Do you wonder what Moses must have thought about as he sat by that well in the desert region of Midian? I imagine the heat and discomfort of the desert made him long for the palace of Pharaoh. But I think he also must have contemplated the reason he had lost it all. In the quietness of that desert, he was forced to come to grips with reality. He had no one to blame but himself. I think that is most painful truth anyone has to face—the fact that some suffering is a result of our own doing.

Moses is not unlike many men who, through one bad decision, lose everything dear to them. For some reason, the mid-life crisis causes many people, especially men, to abandon reason and make unwise choices. All of us have witnessed men who, through unwise investments, lost it all.

Why are people in mid-life prone to make bad decisions? Maybe it's the fear that the end of life is approaching and time is running out to "make their mark." That may have been Moses' motivation. Seeing the suffering of the Hebrews, maybe Moses thought that it was time to do something. If the deliverance of God's people was ever going to take place, it would have to be NOW!

So that you don't think I'm reading something into the text that is not there, look at Acts 7 again:

> But when he was approaching the age of forty, it entered his mind to visit his brethren, the sons of Israel. And when he saw one of them being treated unjustly, he defended him and took vengeance for the oppressed by striking down the Egyptian. And he supposed that his brethren understood that God was granting them deliverance through him; but they did not understand (vv. 23-25).

Notice when the "thought entered his mind." It was at age forty. Moses was getting anxious about God's unfulfilled promise of deliverance. So he decided that he would take things into his own hands. *He* would start the deliverance by killing one of the Egyptians. So he decided to act.

Moses was in the desert, mentally kicking himself for having done such a stupid thing. And yet, at this time in his life, he was most open to listen to God. I think that is one reason God allows us to suffer the consequences of our sins. Only when we are at the end of our rope are we prone to be receptive to God's message. The purpose of God's judgment in the lives of His children is not retribution—that was poured out on Jesus Christ at the cross. God's purpose in discipline is *restoration*.

In ancient times when a field became unproductive and covered with rank growth, it would be burned. Why? To destroy the field? No, to salvage it for future cultivation. It is the same way in the lives of God's people. The fiery judgment of God prepares us for future usefulness. I think that is what the writer of Hebrews had in mind in Hebrews 6:7-8:

> For ground that drinks the rain which often falls upon it and brings forth vegetation useful to those for whose sake it is also tilled, receives a blessing from God; but if it yields thorns and thistles, it is worthless and close to being cursed, and it ends up being burned.

Moses was experiencing the inevitable judgment of God for his actions. But it was out of love that God disciplined him. Again, the writer of Hebrews has an insightful word for us about God's disci-

pline: "For those whom the Lord loves He disciplines . . . All discipline for the moment seems not be joyful, but sorrowful; yet to those
who have been trained by it, afterwards it yields the peaceful fruit of
righteousness" (12:6, 11).

Although he may not have realized it at the time, Moses later wrote
that this desert experience was a time that God ministered to him:
"He found him in a desert land./And in the howling waste of a
wilderness;/He encircled him, He cared for him,/He guarded him as
the pupil of His eye" (Deut. 32:10).

In my mother's Bible these words are written: "The most precious
object of God's love is his child in the desert." Some of you reading
this book are in a "desert" experience. You've blown it. *You*, not
someone else, have made a bad decision. And you are now suffering
the consequences for it. You wonder if God is through with you. Have
you so messed up God's plan for your life that you will never be able
to undo the damage?

The life of Moses should be an encouragement to you. Yes, he had
to pay the consequences of his sin. The law of Galatians 6:7 was in
effect back then as well as now: "Do not be deceived, God is not
mocked; for whatever a man sows, this he will also reap." Christians
are saved from the eternal, not the temporal, consequences of their
sins.

Notice the length of Moses' restoration period—forty years! God
was not finished with Moses yet. In those forty years of desert experience, God taught Moses some important lessons that equipped him
for the greater work that God had for him to do.

Let me point out three truths I believe Moses may have reflected
on during his time in the desert. They are truths that might save you
from a "desert" experience:

The Right Thing Done The Wrong Way Is Wrong.

Let me put it another way: "Spiritual goals are never brought about
by carnal means." God wanted to release the children of Israel from
the Egyptians. That was the right goal, but Moses made the same
mistake that many of us do: He tried to accomplish God's purpose
in his own strength. He went outside one day, got angry over the
mistreatment of the Hebrews, and killed an Egyptian.

I imagine in that millisecond of thought before he struck the Egyptian, Moses rationalized that he was helping God achieve His ultimate purpose. So, what was the problem?

The problem was that "the anger of man does not achieve the righteousness of God" (Jas. 1:20). Anything done out of anger—disciplining your children, correcting an employee, disagreeing in a meeting—is wrong.

Moses apparently had a lifelong problem battling his temper. Remember the incident at Sinai? Moses was receiving the law from God, while the people were waiting for him at the base of the mountain. They decided he was not returning, so they constructed a golden calf to worship and became involved in all types of debauchery. When Moses returned and saw what had happened, he was filled with rage. Look at Exodus 32:19-20:

> And it came about, as soon as Moses came near the camp, that he saw the calf and the dancing; and Moses' anger burned, and he threw the tablets from his hands and shattered them at the foot of the mountain. And he took the calf which they had made and burned it with fire, and ground it to powder, and scattered it over the surface of the water, and made the sons of Israel drink it.

Yecchh! That story reminds me of being in Vacation Bible School as a preschooler. The teacher left the room for a minute, and I led the children in my own form of debauchery. Most of us had lunch boxes with thermoses. I led the other kids in crumbling up our sandwiches, cookies, potato chips, and the like in our thermoses filled with milk or juice. It was great fun—until the teacher returned. To make an example of me—and to discourage any future rebellions—she made me drink every drop of my concoction! I'll assure you that a pimento cheese sandwich, pickles, and chips mixed with chocolate milk tastes no better than the brew Moses made those rebellious Israelites drink!

Moses was mad! Mad enough to throw down the law he had just received from God. Someone might say that it was simply a case of righteous indignation. And there is such a thing (as when Jesus cleansed the Temple). But the point is that Moses had a temper that could be triggered quickly.

Look at Numbers 20. The children of Israel were grumbling about their lack of water. Moses was tired of their constant complaining and asked God for some relief. God told him to speak to the rock and it would bring forth water. Notice that the instruction was only to speak to the rock. God wanted to make it clear to the people that *He* was the one responsible for the miracle.

But out of exasperation and anger, Moses committed a grave error:

> Then Moses lifted up his hand and struck the rock twice with his rod; and water came forth abundantly, and the congregation and their beasts drank. But the Lord said to Moses and Aaron, "Because you have not believed Me, to treat Me as holy in the sight of the sons of Israel, therefore you shall not bring this assembly into the land which I have given them" (vv. 11-12).

Notice the principle here. God wanted to provide the people with water. He gave Moses precise instructions about how He wanted to do it. But Moses again tried to accomplish God's will his way. Because of this sin Moses was prohibited from entering into the Promised Land. The right thing done the wrong way is wrong.

The Right Thing Done at the Wrong Time is Wrong.

As Moses spent his time in the desert reflecting on his killing the Egyptian, I imagine he thought about the importance of timing. God wanted to deliver His people *according to His timetable,* not Moses'. Moses was off by forty years! Many of us make the mistake of trying to push ahead to accomplish God's will without being sensitive to God's timing. Someone has said, "One blow struck when the time is right is worth more than 1,000 struck in premature eagerness."

This principle is true in every aspect of life. For example, you might have a legitimate suggestion or request for your employer. But if you are wise, you will be careful about your timing. It's probably not wise to ask for a raise after the annual report has been released showing that your firm is in the red!

Or, in your marriage, you might have a legitimate suggestion for your spouse. But saying the right thing at the end of a hectic day might cause more misunderstanding and discontent than you experienced before making the suggestion.

Jesus is a perfect example of someone who was sensitive to God's timing. For example, look at this account in John 7:

> After these things Jesus was walking in Galilee; for he was unwilling to walk in Judea, because the Jews were seeking to kill Him. . . . His

brothers therefore said to Him, "Depart from here, and go into Judea, that Your disciples also may behold Your works which You are doing." Jesus therefore said to them, "My time is not yet at hand; . . . Go up to the feast yourselves; I do not go up to this feast because My time has not yet fully come" (vv. 1, 3, 6-8).

Jesus was not afraid of dying. But He knew His death had to be at God's time in order to have fulfilled the prophecies about Messiah.

As important as knowing the "what" of God's will is knowing the "when."

The Right Objective Accomplished in the Right Way at the Right Time Brings Honor to God.

Notice the big mistake Moses made: "So he looked this way and that, and when he saw there was no one around he struck down the Egyptian and hid him in the sand" (Ex. 2:12).

You can see Moses quickly looking to the left and to the right. The mistake he made was not looking *up* to see what God thought. The result was not the exodus Moses hoped to accomplish but a murdered Egyptian and a flight from the authorities!

Now, compare that to what happened forty years later when Moses followed God's plan and timing for delivering His people:

> Thus the Lord saved Israel that day from the land of the Egyptians, and Israel saw the Egyptians dead on the seashore. And when Israel saw the great power which the Lord had used against the Egyptians, the people feared the Lord, and they believed in the Lord and in His servant Moses (Ex. 14:30-31).

You no doubt have heard the saying: "There is no limit to the good a person can do, if he is willing to let someone else take the credit." When we are willing to let God take the credit for what He does through us, there is no limit to what He will do through us!

Back to the Desert

Can we know the turning point in Moses' life? I think it occurred in this desert experience. Moses had to choose how to respond in his mid-life crisis to God's discipline. He chose to accept God's discipline and learn from it. He chose to look toward a future of useful service to God. The result?

Now it came about in the course of those many days that the King of Egypt died. And the sons of Israel sighed because of the bondage, and they cried out; and their cry for help because of their bondage rose up to God. So God heard their groanings; and God remembered His covenant with Abraham, Isaac, and Jacob (Ex. 2:23-24).

After *many* days, God was ready to deliver His people from Egypt. And who would He use to do that? That servant of His in the desert. The one others had forgotten. The man who surely thought God had forgotten him. The man who had come through the discipline of God wiser and stronger than before.

You have the same choice about how to respond to mid-life crises. You can give up your old dreams and not dream new dreams, or you can use your crises as times of learning more about yourself and God.

5
Hannah
Dedicating Your Best

I don't think I fully comprehended the gospel message until I become a parent. Although I could recite John 3:16 backwards and had never missed a Lord's Supper service, the concept of a father's sacrificing his only son for the welfare of others escaped my understanding. My wife and I recently became proud parents of a precious baby girl named Julia. With my first glimpse of Julia, my life took on a new meaning. As in the proverbial "falling-in-love" experience, colors became brighter and sounds became sharper—my coffee even tasted "coffeeer"! Now I am convinced that there is nothing as cute as a little baby—*my* baby. I find myself dropping in unexpectedly at the church nursery just to be sure the teachers are treating Julia right, only to run into my wife, who is on a similar mission! Even the thought of Julia's suffering a chigger bite disturbs me greatly.

Would I ever entertain the thought of permitting her to suffer for someone else's sake? Of course not! She is not only the best that life has to offer but also a part of me. Being a parent makes me more amazed that God would allow His only Son to suffer and die for my sins.

In many ways, the story of Hannah and her son, Samuel, is a type of the gospel. For Hannah chose to relinquish her only son to God's service before Samuel was even conceived. Her dedication to the Lord was accentuated by the fact that Samuel was the son she had begged God for after many years of being barren. We wonder where she found the inner strength to part with a son she had longed for. And it's amazing to think that she parted with him the first day she felt he could survive without her. The story of this woman who dedicated her best to God is found in 1 Samuel 1—2.

Hannah: The "Barrenness" of Ephraim

What woman would feel elated if her husband introduced her to his business associates as his "favorite wife"? Would such a compliment evoke only a blushing protest from his wife? In my house, it would trigger a summons to the divorce court! Yet the title "favorite wife" was the dubious honor that Hannah enjoyed as the first—but barren —wife of Elkanah the Ephraimite. Although bigamy was not sanctioned by God, the Hebrew husband of an infertile wife often took a second wife in order to bear sons to protect his posterity. This practice was especially prevalent during Hannah's time—the lawless time of the judges when "everyone did what was right in his own eyes" (Judg. 21:25).

Hannah was a woman with thoughts and feelings, not merely a respected character who graces the pages of the Old Testament. She may have been tall and graceful with dark skin. Although the Bible does not tell us what she looked like, it does tell us that she was very unhappy because she was barren. I wonder how Hannah felt the day that Elkanah decided to take another wife to make up for her weakness. Was this decision made on a balmy Monday morning or on a chilly Friday night? Did Hannah cry herself to sleep that night, or did she stoically step out into the night air to walk and walk, tempted never to return home?

And how did Hannah feel at the wedding ceremony between her husband and Penninah? Was Hannah matron of honor at her husband's wedding or merely a member of the house party? What were Hannah's reactions the day that Penninah, the "other woman," moved into Hannah's home to begin an intimate relationship with Elkanah? Did Hannah have to force a smile as she met Penninah at the door, or did she find an errand to do so someone else could form the welcoming committee? Did Hannah have to make closet space, as well as sleeping space, for her rival?

We do not know the details; we can only imagine the awkwardness of the situation. But we do know that Hannah had to open up her heart, as well as her home, to a cruel woman who taunted Hannah mercilessly.

"This Year in Shiloh"

The Scripture says that Hannah's "rival" would provoke her, especially on their annual trip to Shiloh to make sacrifices to the Lord: "Her rival, however, would provoke her bitterly to irritate her, because the Lord had closed her womb. And it happened year after year, as often as she went up to the house of the Lord, she would provoke her, so she wept and would not eat" (1 Sam. 1:6-7).

How Hannah must have dreaded those trips! Maybe she had to hop onto a camel with Penninah's kids for a dusty, fifteen-mile journey, only to meet with her rival's jabs at the end of her trip. We can imagine her wearily bumping along, sandwiched between two adolescents who argued endlessly. During those times, her thoughts probably turned to the Lord, and she may have wondered why He had chosen this plan for her life. Hadn't she been faithful to Him throughout her lifetime? Wasn't He a rewarder of the righteous? As she mused about her predicament and meditated upon His promises, she became more and more determined to again ask Him for a son who would fulfill her heart's deepest desire. She determined, *Yes, it will be different this year in Shiloh!*

In 1 Samuel 1:8-10, we see that it was not enough for Hannah to be Elkanah's "favorite wife," she desired to have a child of her own:

> Then Elkanah her husband said to her, "Hannah, why do you weep and why do you not eat and why is your heart sad? Am I not better to you than ten sons? Then Hannah rose after eating and drinking in Shiloh. Now Eli the priest was sitting on the seat by the doorpost of the temple of the Lord. And she, greatly distressed, prayed to the Lord and wept bitterly.

Hannah's barren womb had created a barren life. She longed to rejoice with the psalmist, who declared: "I would have despaired unless/I had believed that I would see the goodness of the Lord/In the land of the living" (Ps. 27:13). As a woman of faith, Hannah believed God's promises about the afterlife, but she wanted some reward and fulfillment in her earthly life as well. She desired to touch the tiny fingers and kiss the soft face of a baby—*her* baby.

We can all relate to Hannah's desire to experience God's blessings in this lifetime. As Christians, we are grateful for our salvation, and we eagerly await heaven. But as creatures who can touch, taste, see, hear, and smell, we desire an abundant life now. And what more natural desire is there than that of a woman for a child? In Hannah's day, the absence of children was considered a curse.

Hannah's Request

The way that Hannah turned to the Lord to fulfill her desire is significant. She did not approach Him in the bored, mindless way that a present-day believer might offer a prayer during a Wednesday night prayer meeting: "Oh Lord, *(yawn, scratch)* please bless my dog, my goldfish, the preacher, and all others who are tired, have allergies, ingrown toenails, etc." Instead, she approached Him with weeping and with such torment of soul that only her lips moved, causing Eli, the priest, to accuse her of being drunk!

Notice also the vow accompanying her request. She desired a son so strongly that she was willing to give him to someone else to rear. Before he was conceived, she dedicated him to the Lord:

> She made a vow and said, "Oh Lord of hosts, if Thou wilt indeed look on the affliction of Thy maidservant and remember me, and not forget Thy maidservant, but wilt give Thy maidservant a son, then I will give him to the Lord all the days of his life, and a razor shall never come on his head" (1 Sam. 1:11).

In her prayer, she referred to the Nazirite vow (Num. 6:1-8), which is the same vow that Samson's parents had made under similar circumstances (Judg. 13:2-5). Hannah vowed not only to forgive her child to the Lord, but also to give him up "all the days of his life"— FOREVER!

As I read these verses, I marvel at Hannah's faith. Not only did she turn him over to the priests of Shiloh once he was weaned but also she limited her "visitation rights" to several times a year when the family journeyed to Shiloh. On one of these visits, she would bring him a robe that she had made for him during the previous year. Can you imagine seeing your preschooler only several times a year because of a limitation YOU had prescribed? You would have to miss all of his "firsts": his first day of school, his first bicycle, his first sleepover with a friend. How could Hannah bear such a sacrifice?

Shiloh Song

Hannah's sacrifice was the result of her strong faith in the sovereignty of God, as expressed in her song of praise which is recorded in 1 Samuel 2:1-10. The timing of this praise prayer is just as significant as the content. She expressed her faith in God *after* she relinquished her son to God, rather than at his conception or birth.

Let's look at life from Hannah's position for a moment. Suppose that, as a female in ancient Jewish society, your entire self-image, usefulness to society, and purpose of living were governed by your fertility. You were unable to conceive. Finally, after years of begging God for a child, you became pregnant. Wouldn't this be an appropriate time to praise God? Or, maybe you would wait until the child was born, thanking Him for the miracle of new life.

The time that Hannah chose to offer one of the most beautiful poems of thanksgiving was after she relinquished her child. Her poem is uniquely trusting in content, as well as in timing. In this song of praise, we understand that Hannah was able to trust God with her son because she understood the character of God.

At the beginning of the song, we hear her joyous attitude in the words: "My heart exults in the Lord" (1 Sam. 2:1). She then proceeded to delineate the attributes that made Him trustworthy. First, she cited His unique holiness in her statement: "There is no one holy like the Lord" (1 Sam. 2:2). Secondly, she praised His strength and immutability: "Nor is there any rock like our God" (1 Sam. 2:2). She praised God for His vast knowledge and discernment: "For the Lord is a God of knowledge, And with Him actions are weighed" (1 Sam. 2:3). Next, she dwelled on His power, as demonstrated in her life: "Even the barren gives birth" (1 Sam. 2:5).

Not only had the Lord demonstrated power in her life but also He was in control of every life (1 Sam. 2:6-8). Finally, Hannah warned of God's judgment of the wicked, in contrast to His preservation of the godly: "He keeps the feet of His godly ones, But the wicked ones are silenced in darkness" (1 Sam. 2:9). What did that have to do with her son, Samuel? Samuel was to be raised in the household of Eli, the priest. Eli was old and blind. Furthermore, his sons, Hopni and Phinehas, were reprobates—keeping company with the prostitutes of Shiloh. It was not a great environment for an infant! Yet Hannah believed that the Lord who "keeps the feet of His godly ones" would be able to keep Samuel from harm in her absence. And that's exactly what happened. The Bible says that during that time "Samuel grew and the Lord was with him and let none of his words fall" (1 Sam. 3:19).

As I look at the life of Hannah, I see three truths about worshiping God:

Worshiping God Involves Giving.

Notice in 1 Samuel 1:3 that Elkanah went to Shiloh yearly "to worship and to sacrifice." There is an inseparable link between worship and sacrifice. Worship is not just a spiritual feeling we try to conjure up. Instead, worship demands a response—a sacrifice. That sacrifice might be our money, our time, or our obedience.

Worshiping God Involves Giving Our Best.

God is not interested in our leftovers. "If I have any money left at the end of the month, I'll give it to God." Or, "If I have time, I'll pray and read God's Word." God wants the "firstfruits" of our money, time, and our affections. David said it this way: "I will not offer burnt offerings to the Lord my God which cost me nothing" (2 Sam. 24:24). For Hannah, giving her best meant giving her son to God.

Worshiping God Involves Giving Our Best Unconditionally.

Today, we have many false teachers who say, "If you give to God, He will reward you tenfold!" In other words, if I give my money to God, He will give it back with interest. If that is true, my gift to God is not a sacrifice but simply a good investment!

When we give sacrificially to God, we give with no strings attached. For example, if you give a relationship to God, it means you have no expectations. If God wants to bless it, fine. But if He wants to end it, that's all right, too.

Does God reward us for our sacrifices? Yes, but it is not always in the way we imagine. Hannah gave Samuel to God, with the full expectation that he would belong to the priestly service forever. And he did. But God rewarded Hannah by giving her five other children!

Giving her son to the Lord marked a crossroads in Hannah's life. She could have continued weeping about her lot in life, failing to trust

God with her circumstances. Instead, she chose to give up something that she had not yet received from the Lord. As a result of her faith, Hannah received a son who was destined to usher in a new, more God-fearing era in Israel's history.

You may be facing a crossroads experience today. There may be something you have refused to give to the Lord for fear of what might happen: your business, your family, or your possessions. If so, there is some encouragement for you in the story of Hannah. Her life demonstrates the truth that God is a rewarder of those who diligently seek Him.

6
Ruth
Remaining Faithful Despite the Cost

After becoming a Christian, Jack Eckerd, head of the tremendous drug store empire, went into one of his stores and saw pornographic magazines being sold. He called one of his vice presidents and asked how much money they made selling those magazines. The vice president said they brought in a profit of three million dollars annually. Eckerd ordered them removed from every store. Faithfulness to Christ can mean severe financial loss. But sometimes faithfulness exacts an even greater cost—the loss of one's family.

Faithfulness: The Crossroads

Ruth was a young woman who chose to remain faithful to God, despite the cost. Ruth inspires us because, when she came to a crossroad in her life, she chose to follow the Lord's people, thereby following Him.

As the Moabite widow of a Hebrew, Ruth faced a turning point. Would she return to her native country to remarry and produce children, or would she follow her aging mother-in-law to a foreign land? Her mother-in-law's suggestion forced a choice: "Naomi said to her two daughters-in-law, 'Go, return each of you to her mother's house. May the Lord deal kindly with you as you have dealt with the dead and with me. May the Lord grant that you may find rest, each in the house of her husband' " (Ruth 1:8-9).

Faithfulness: The Cost

Ruth gave up all that was meaningful to follow the Lord. And she inspires us in how easily she gave up these things, in how quickly she turned to follow Him, in spite of strong pressure to fulfill her own desires. Although Ruth's sister-in-law immediately returned to her pagan land, Ruth clung to her mother-in-law, despite Naomi's contrary urging:

> "Behold, your sister-in-law has gone back to her people and her gods; return after your sister-in-law." But Ruth said, "Do not urge me to leave you or turn back from following you; for where you go, I will go, and where you lodge, I will lodge. Your people shall be my people, and your God, my God. Where you die, I will die, and there will I be buried. Thus may the Lord do to me, and worse, if anything but death parts you and me" (Ruth 1:15-17).

Ruth's dedication reminds me of the dedication Jesus demanded of His disciples: "If any one wishes to come after Me, let him deny himself, and take up his cross, and follow Me. For whoever wishes to save his life shall lose it; but whoever loses his life for My sake shall find it" (Matt. 16:24-25).

What did Ruth lose by following her mother-in-law to Judah?

Her Native Land

Ruth's loss of her native land may not seem significant because Moab sounds like the kind of place where women wrap their faces with black gauze to furtively dart down brick-paved alleys, balancing clay pots on their heads—the kind of place where drums beat dully at dusk and coyotes shriek shrilly at midnight. Who would *want* to live in Moab? The answer: a Moabitess—who *likes* black gauze, head pots, beating drums, and shrieking coyotes! As a Moabitess, Ruth relinquished all that was familiar—customs, dress, food, and housing—many earthly things that make a person feel secure.

Her Family

Naomi urged Ruth to return to her "mother's house" (Ruth 1:8). I think that suggestion has universal appeal. Even most married adults with children of their own enjoy visiting their parents; there is nothing as comforting as being surrounded by people who know you fully and love you unconditionally, even if you *can't* agree on a thermostat setting! And there is nothing so soothing as the presence of familiar objects—be it a stately grandfather clock or a humble electric toaster. The security found in the relationships and the environment of home would be especially welcomed in Ruth's predicament—a time of grief.

Remarriage

Ruth did not live in a time where mates were found anywhere and everywhere. She could not become a contestant on a television dating show. She could not cruise down the local drag in a yellow convertible, checking out the action. Instead, Ruth lived in an era of arranged marriages. And the men in Judah, her chosen destination, had been warned about foreign women like herself: "You shall make no covenant with them or with their gods. They shall not live in your land, lest they make you sin against Me; for if you serve their gods, it will surely be a snare to you" (Ex. 23:32-33). In choosing to follow Naomi, Ruth was turning her back on remarriage.

Children

Ruth, like many faithful Old Testament women, was barren. And, without a husband, she would be destined to remain barren for life. To appreciate Ruth's dedication, we must remember that in her day life revolved around the family. Ruth could not choose to pursue a Ph.D. in aerospace engineering or an executive position with Price Waterhouse in place of rearing children. A relationship with a bitter, grieving mother-in-law and a residence in a strange land was all that could compensate for her loss. Or was it?

Faithfulness: The Cause

What caused Ruth to remain faithful to her bitter mother-in-law, despite the enormous personal cost? The biblical account does not detail Ruth's life as the Gentile wife of a Hebrew. But her immediate and unswerving decision to assume Naomi's people and God indicates that she knew something of Jehovah. Naomi's household must have been one where the Scriptures were read and where the God of the Scriptures was worshiped. Ruth had grown to appreciate the security the Hebrew people found in the one true God: Jehovah.

Ruth was willing to deny her desires in order to follow this strange God because she, like the psalmist, knew that His "lovingkindness is better than life" (Ps. 63:3). She knew that God could compensate for the loss of country, family, marriage, and children. We can all benefit from lessons found in Ruth's unswerving commitment to God:

A Relationship with God Supercedes Patriotism.

In Ruth's faithfulness, we have a lesson in believer's citizenship. Ruth realized, as did the many Old Testament saints listed in Hebrews 11, that those who believe in the Lord must live as "strangers and exiles on the earth" (v. 13). Her decision to follow Naomi indicates that she desired that "better," "heavenly" country enjoyed after death (v. 16). Through Ruth's example, we are encouraged to put our heavenly citizenship above our earthly citizenship.

A Relationship with God Supercedes Family Loyalty.

In the same way that believers are citizens of a better country than any found on earth, believers are also members of a higher family structure. Although God designed and ordained the family, Jesus also stated: "If anyone comes to Me, and does not hate his own father and mother and wife and children and brothers and sisters, yes, and even his own life, he cannot be My disciple" (Luke 14:26).

In both of these concepts—the higher country and the higher family—we encounter the more profound concept of the higher life. When Ruth followed Naomi, she chose the godly life over the ungodly life. Ruth would have agreed with the psalmist who declared: "For a day in Thy courts is better than a thousand outside./I would rather stand at the threshold of the house of my God,/Than dwell in the tents of wickedness" (84:10).

Having lived for several years in a Hebrew family, Ruth would have been familiar with Moses, the Hebrew who chose "to endure ill-treatment with the people of God, [rather] than to enjoy the passing pleasures of sin; considering the reproach of Christ greater riches than the treasures of Egypt; for he was looking to the reward" (Heb. 11:25-26).

Therefore, when Ruth turned her back on her family in the heathen country of Moab in order to follow Naomi to the godly country of Judah, she was making a decision between good and evil. She knew, from the testimony of those who had gone before her, that God would reward her choice.

A Relationship with God Supercedes Matrimony.

Although marriage is ordained by God, it is a blessing that some believers must forfeit if they are to follow Him fully. Even those of us who enjoy a marriage relationship also enjoy the higher relationship with Christ, who understands and loves us with unlimited capacity. Even married believers can agree with the psalmist, who declared: "Whom have I in heaven but thee?/And besides Thee, I desire nothing on earth" (73:25).

Ruth realized that a relationship with God superceded matrimony, especially with an ungodly Moabite.

A Relationship with God Supercedes Parenthood.

Because children are life itself, many people place their children first in their lives. As new parents, my wife and I were forced to leave our baby daughter with a friend for a couple of days because we were too ill to care for her. As we apologized profusely for this intrusion, our friend interrupted and said, "You don't understand. I love to watch her. She laughs, she coos, she gurgles . . . She is *life!*" Children rejuvenate us. And yet even the sparkle of children pales in the brilliance of eternal life—the quality of life believers enjoy on earth.

I think Ruth understood a timeless principle that was later declared by Jesus in the New Testament: "And everyone who has left houses or brothers or sisters or father or mother or children or farms for My name's sake, shall receive many times as much, and shall inherit eternal life" (Matt. 19:29).

Ruth trusted God to open her womb if He desired. But, more importantly, she was completely fulfilled in the quality of life available through a relationship with Him.

The lessons learned from Ruth's decision to follow God, despite great personal cost, are so rich that her story could end with her decision to follow Naomi, and readers of the Bible would be blessed. But thankfully for Ruth, this was merely the beginning of her story!

In time the Lord blessed her with the very things she was willing to sacrifice. In future events of Ruth's life, we see an affirmation of the psalmist's promise, "No good thing does He withhold from those who walk uprightly" (84:11).

Faithfulness: the Circumstances

It happened this way: once upon a barley-gleaning time . . .

Ruth and her mother-in-law, Naomi, traveled to Bethlehem, searching for food during widespread famine. In God's providence, Ruth started gleaning barley in the field of Boaz, one of Naomi's nearest relatives. And, also in God's providence, Boaz took a liking to Ruth and gave her special privileges. Did Boaz admire Ruth's beauty, wit, ambition, or spunk? No, he admired her humble faithfulness. They conferred one afternoon in Boaz's barley field. The conversation might have gone something like this:

Ruth: "Why are you partial to me, especially since I am a foreigner?"

Boaz: "I've heard through the grapevine about your commitment to your mother-in-law after your husband's death. I'm impressed that you left your native country to come here. May God bless your commitment."

Boaz's favor toward Ruth lasted through the end of the barley harvest and into the wheat harvest (Ruth 2:23), giving Naomi plenty of time to devise a matchmaking scheme.

When Naomi sensed that the time was as ripe as the wheat, she suggested that Ruth assume a more aggressive role:

> Then Naomi her mother-in-law said to her, "My daughter, shall I not seek security for you, that it may be well with you? And now is not Boaz our kinsman, with whose maids you were? Behold, he winnows barley at the threshing floor tonight. Wash yourself therefore, and anoint yourself and put on your best clothes, and go down to the threshing floor; but do not make yourself known to the man until he has finished eating and drinking. And it shall be when he lies down, that you shall notice the place where he lies, and you shall go and uncover his feet and lie down; then he will tell you what you shall do" (Ruth 3:1-4).

Now, Naomi wasn't stupid. She chose barley-winnowing day as the perfect time to approach Boaz. After an entire day of partying and gleefully throwing grain in the air, the full-tummied Boaz, a confirmed bachelor, might be more open to assuming a wife. And a little soap, perfume, and frills never hindered romance. Without protesting, dutiful Ruth followed Naomi's instructions.

Now, we already know that Ruth's dedication to Naomi impressed Boaz. But, naturally, Ruth's desire to become his wife impressed Boaz even more!

> Then he said, "May you be blessed of the Lord, my daughter. You have shown your last kindness to be better than the first by not going after young men, whether poor or rich. And now, my daughter, do not fear. I will do for you whatever you ask, for all my people in the city know that you are a woman of excellence" (Ruth 3:10-11).

No wonder Boaz did not decline Ruth's marriage invitation! He recognized her as a "woman of excellence"—the kind of superwoman delineated in Proverbs 31. Apparently, Ruth was not only faithful, she was the kind of woman who stays up until 4:30 AM stitching linen long johns, yet can still smile demurely from the head table of a barley-growers luncheon at noon. And she was not only tireless in her labor, but she was also young enough that Boaz called her his daughter! Boaz, the astute businessman, knew a good deal when it came his way!

But Boaz saw one hitch in his business transaction: Naomi had one relative closer than he (Ruth 3:12). How would this development affect their marriage plans? Under the levirate law, a barren widow was to marry her deceased husband's brother in order to bear a son in her husband's honor. (Deut. 25:5-10). Because Ruth's brother-in-law was deceased, the law permitted his next closest relative to marry her in his place. Boaz was a close relative, but there was an even closer relative.

Providentially, the closer relative was unable to marry Ruth, so she became Boaz's wife: "So Boaz took Ruth, and she became his wife, and he went in to her. And the Lord enabled her to conceive, and she gave birth to a son" (Ruth 4:13).

Ruth received a husband and a son and a place in the history of the strange land she inhabited, not to mention eternal spiritual fame. The son whom she bore became the father of Jesse, who became the father of David. Ultimately, Christ came from this lineage. This barren widow's blessings developed from her sacrificial choice, which led her to the right field . . . once upon a barley-gleaning time.

Faithfulness: The Connection

Well, what a nice story. Girl meets boy, girl gets boy—maybe they even fall in love when they get to know one another better. But this story lacks something. Frankly, it's not very exciting.

That's exactly the point! God uses this story to show that He values the sterling, yet uncelebrated, quality of faithfulness. You see, there is nothing exciting about . . .

—a couple who has been married for fifty years.

—a citizen who votes at every election.

—a church member with perfect Sunday School attendance.

—a preacher whose life is above reproach (1 Tim. 3:2).

—a virtuous woman (Prov. 31).

And there is certainly nothing exciting about a young widow who follows her mother-in-law around. These people make many moderns yawn. The unfaithful celebrities revealed in the tabloids are much more fascinating!

Not only is it boring to observe the faithful but also it's boring to *be* faithful! How we dread Mondays . . . overtime . . . inventory . . . routine reports . . . dirty dishes . . . cooking supper . . . paying bills . . . taking exams. Yet, how we anticipate Fridays . . . coffee breaks . . . vacations . . . eating out . . . payday . . . spring break! We all look forward to relief from drudgery, whatever the form.

Ruth's story, however, gives a new angle on living with drudgery. She learned the secret of living with drudgery—how to "dwell in the land and cultivate faithfulness" (Ps. 37:3). She learned how not merely to accept, but even thrive in her daily circumstances.

Ruth's life was not fascinating. Barley gleaning was probably not much more exciting than traveling with a bitter mother-in-law. And marrying an old man was probably only a tad more fascinating than barley gleaning, even if she did get to throw herself at his feet in complete abandon, adorned in her best!

We could try to say that Ruth was faithful because Ruth lived in "the good old days" when people had strong morals, family ties, and commitment to God-given institutions. But that would not be true. Instead, Ruth lived in the lawless time of the judges, when "everyone did what was right in his own eyes" (Judg. 21:25). Paradoxically,

Ruth was a maverick in her faithfulness, having come from a faithless, ungodly background.

I think that the secret of Ruth's faithfulness was that she put her life at the mercy of a faithful God. She was willing to give up religion, community, family, marriage, and children because she trusted God's faithfulness. And she was not disappointed.

7
David
Healing a Guilty Conscience

Years ago a favorite television program was "This is Your Life." At the beginning of the show, the host Ralph Edwards, approached some unsuspecting person and said, "This is your life!" For the next thirty minutes, the host recounted various incidents from the person's life. Different personalities from the person's past—grade-school teachers, employers, old boyfriends or girlfriends—were brought on stage to relate interesting, and often embarrassing, incidents from the person's life. You could tell by watching the guest's face that he would have preferred that some things be left out. But millions of Americans delighted in seeing some poor soul humiliated every week!

Let's pretend that you were to be a guest on "This is Your Life" today. For thirty minutes your life would be reviewed before millions of people—both friends and strangers. Would you be willing to participate? Can you think of things in your life about which you would rather no one knew?

The story is told of a prominent playwright in London who sent the following anonymous note as a joke to twenty of London's leading citizens: "All has been found out. Leave town at once." All twenty left London immediately!

All of us have certain things in our lives of which we are ashamed. The Bible calls such a feeling a guilty conscience, and a guilty conscience can have devastating consequences. One psychiatrist said that 70 percent of people in mental wards could be released today if they knew how to find forgiveness. Guilt not only causes emotional stress but also breaks our relationship with God. In 1 Timothy 1:18-19, Paul said that two things are necessary to live the Christian life: faith and a clear conscience. "Fight the good fight, keeping faith and a good conscience, which some have rejected and suffered shipwreck in regard to their faith."

Are you suffering from a guilty conscience? Are things in your past, or maybe things you are involved in right now, hurting your relationship with God? If so, how do you get rid of a guilty conscience? The answers can be discovered by looking at the one person in the Bible who had the best reason to feel guilty of anyone I know. Yet, he found God's way of handling guilt. The story of this man's sin, guilt, and forgiveness is found in 2 Samuel 11:1 to 12:23 and Psalm 51.

The Scarlet King

The inscription at the beginning of Psalm 51 reads, "A psalm of David, when Nathan the prophet came to him, after he had gone into Bathsheba" (NASB, RSV). David was the king of Israel. He had the most dazzling rule of any king in Israel's history. He was a righteous king. The Bible says that he was a man after God's own heart. But toward the end of his reign, he fell into the double sin of adultery and murder.

> Then it happened in the spring, at the time when kings go out to battle, that David sent Joab and his servants with him and all Israel, and they destroyed the sons of Ammon and besieged Rabbah. But David stayed at Jerusalem. Now when evening came David arose from his bed and walked around on the roof of the king's house, and from the roof he saw a woman bathing; and the woman was very beautiful in appearance. So David sent and inquired about the woman. And one said, "Is this not Bathsheba, the daughter of Eliam, the wife of Uriah the Hittite?" And David sent messengers and took her, and when she came to him, he lay with her; and when she had purified herself from her uncleanness, she returned to her house. And the woman conceived; and she sent and told David, and said, "I am pregnant" (2 Sam. 11:1-5).

David should have been in battle with his men. Instead, his idle hands (and thoughts!) gave the enemy an opportunity. By human law, the king could have any woman he wanted, but according to God's law, David was guilty of adultery. Being a godly man did not exempt him from God's law: "Whatever a man sows, this he will also reap" (Gal. 6:7). In David's case, his "sowing" resulted in Bathsheba's pregnancy.

When Bathsheba told him she was pregnant, David was terrified that someone would find out, so he tried to cover up. He ordered Uriah home from battle, thinking he would surely sleep with his wife, and people would say Uriah was the father of the baby. But it didn't work out as David planned.

> Then David said to Uriah, "Go down to your house, and wash your feet." And Uriah went out of the king's house and a present from the king was sent out after him. But Uriah slept at the door of the king's house with all the servants of his lord, and did not go down to his house (2 Sam. 11:8-9).

Now, for Plan #2

David was now a desperate man. So he devised a plan to have Uriah killed so he might take Bathsheba as his own wife:

> Now it came about in the morning that David wrote a letter to Joab, and sent it by the hand of Uriah. And he had written in the letter, saying, "Place Uriah in the front line of the fiercest battle and withdraw from him, so that he may be struck down and die." Now when the wife of Uriah heard that Uriah her husband was dead, she mourned for her husband. When the time of mourning was over, David sent and brought her to his house and she became his wife; then she bore him a son. But the thing that David had done was evil in the sight of the Lord (2 Sam. 11:14-15, 26-27).

David thought that his secret was safe! *What a clever guy I am! No wonder I am king,* he must have thought to himself. The only problem was that "the thing that David had done was evil in the sight of the Lord."

Days went by—months went by—and nothing adverse happened to David. *Maybe God didn't think this was such a big deal after all,* David must have reasoned to himself. *The kingdom is prospering, I'm enjoying my honey, and I haven't been struck by lightning. Who says "sin doesn't pay?"*

But David was making the same mistake many of us make in our thinking about sin and judgment. We think that just because there is not an immediate judgment of our sin God must not be paying attention to what we do. Or maybe, God has bigger things to worry about than our minor imperfections. We fail to realize that one reason God waits to execute judgment is in order to give us an opportunity to repent and escape His punishment. But we make the mistake of confusing God's patience with God's tolerance of sin. The writer of Eccelesiastes put it this way: "Because the sentence against an evil deed is not executed quickly, therefore the hearts of the sons of men among them are given fully to do evil" (Eccl. 8:11).

The Prophet

After about six months, Nathan, the prophet of God, visited David. He told David a story about a rich man who took the only possession of a poor man, a little ewe lamb, and served it for dinner. "Then David's anger burned greatly against the man, and he said to Nathan, 'As the Lord lives, surely the man who has done this deserves to die. And he must make restitution for the lamb fourfold, because he did this thing and had no compassion' " (2 Sam. 12:5-6).

When David heard the story of this great injustice, he became angry and demanded to know the name of the rich man, so justice could be done. After a pause, Nathan pointed his bony finger at David and said, "You are the man!" Instantly, David's sin was made public.

I think this was a crossroads in David's life. He had a choice to make. He could either continue to deny his sin or he could confess it. He could either try to cover over his sin himself or he could let God deal with his sin. He chose the latter. After confessing his sin before God and before the people, he penned Psalm 51. In it, David expressed some great truths about the way to find relief from a guilty conscience.

How to Overcome Guilt

Realize God Is Not Mad at You

God is not some ogre in heaven with a two by four, waiting to knock us over the head the first time we sin. God loves us. That is what David expressed in the first verse of this psalm: "Be gracious to me, O God, according to Thy loving kindness;/According to the greatness of Thy compassion/blot out my transgressions (51:1).

Notice the words David used to describe God's nature. "gracious," "lovingkindness," "compassion." God deals with His children out of love and compassion. Sin never changes God's attitude toward us.

But sin does break our relationship with God. How? Sin always produces guilt. And guilt breaks a relationship between two people. A relationship can be broken when just one person feels guilty. For example, have you ever talked about someone behind his back and then felt uncomfortable around him? He might not even know what you've done, but you feel guilty and don't want to be around him.

When I was in the first grade, I received my first report card. On the left hand side were my grades for the academic subjects—*As, Bs,* and a few *Cs*. On the right side were the grades for behavior, attitude, and so on. The teacher would either use an *S* for satisfactory or a *U* for unsatisfactory. I never will forget the horror I felt seeing all of those *Ss* and *Us*. You see, I didn't understand a lot about grading. But I knew that *A* was the best you could do and the further you proceeded down the alphabet, the worse it got. If an *F* was enough to fail you, *S* and *U* would probably put you in prison! So I hid my report card from my parents for three days! I remember feeling uncomfortable around them—avoiding them whenever possible. Why? Because I felt so guilty. In reality, they weren't mad at me. But my guilty feelings broke our fellowship.

That reminds me of the story of the husband and wife who were driving to dinner one evening. The wife started to complain, "Honey, when we first married we sat so close together in the car. Now look at all the distance between us. What's happened?" The husband replied, "Dear, I haven't moved!"

God hasn't moved either. He is not mad at us. How do I know? Look at Colossians 1:21-22: "Although you were formerly alienated and hostile in mind, engaged in evil deeds, yet He has now reconciled you in His fleshly body through death, in order to present you before Him holy and blameless and beyond reproach." How does God see a Christian? "Holy, blameless, and beyond reproach!" The first step in gaining a clear conscience is to realize that God is not mad at you.

Ask for God's Forgiveness

David asked for God's forgiveness. He acknowledged his sin. "Wash me thoroughly from my iniquity,/And cleanse me from my sin./For I know my transgressions,/And my sin is ever before me./Against Thee, Thee only, I have sinned,/And done what is evil in Thy sight" (Ps. 51:2-4).

All of us have to deal with our sin. The human way of dealing with sin is to rationalize it or to try to forget about it, hoping it will go away. David tried doing that for awhile, but it didn't work.

In Psalm 32:3-5, David described the results of unconfessed sin in his life which included depression, sleepless nights, and loss of health: "When I kept silent about my sin, my body wasted away/Through my groaning all day long./For day and night Thy hand was heavy upon me;/My vitality was drained away as with the fever-heat of summer."

Just feeling sorry for your sin (or for the consequences of your sin) is not enough. Plenty of people feel remorse without ever asking for God's forgiveness. Sorrow that does not lead to repentance is useless. That's the point Paul made in 2 Corinthians 7:10: "For the sorrow that is according to the will of God produces a repentance without regret, leading to salvation; but the sorrow of the world produces death." David was filled with sorrow, but it was the sorrow "of the world." No amount of tears could atone for David's sin.

God alone is able to cleanse a person from sin. Paul explained this fact further in Colossians 2:13-14. In Paul's day, if you were arrested and put in jail, a certificate was placed over your cell listing your offenses. Look at what happens to our "certificate of debt."

> And when you were dead in your transgressions and the uncircumcision of your flesh, He made you alive together with Him, having forgiven us all our transgressions, having cancelled out the certificate of debt consisting of decrees against us and which was hostile to us; and He has taken it out of the way, having nailed it to the cross.

Our certificate of debt was nailed to the cross! That's the significance of some of Jesus' final words on the cross: "It is finished!" (John 19:30). Literally, that word "finished" means "paid in full." The death of Christ accomplished what nothing else could—the complete and final payment for our sins.

How can I have my sins paid for? The same way David had his sins removed—by asking God for His forgiveness. The Bible says, "If we confess our sins, He is faithful and righteous to forgive us of our sins and to cleanse us from all unrighteousness" (1 John 1:9). If you want forgiveness, all you have to do is ask for it!

Refuse to Allow Satan to Make You Feel Guilty

Once you have asked forgiveness, you can expect Satan to continue to make you feel guilty. You'll be trying to move ahead spiritually, and Satan will grab you by the nape of the neck and say, "Where do you think you're going? Don't you remember what you've done? Why do you think God can use you?"

But an amazing truth about God's forgiveness is this: When God forgives, He forgets! Psalm 103:12 says, "As far as the east is from the west,/So far has He removed our transgressions from us"! Micah 7:19 says, "He casts "all their sins/Into the depths of the sea." Corrie ten Boom, that great saint of God, added these words to that verse: "And He places a sign there that says, 'No Fishing!' "

Think about it! When God forgives us, it is as if the transgression had never taken place! That was the truth David was expressing in Psalm 51:9, "Hide Thy face from my sins,/And blot out all my iniquities." Forgiveness, to David, meant the erasure of sin from God's mind.

Make Restitution Where Needed

Sometimes the nature of our sin requires that we do something besides just asking for God's forgiveness. David had to confess his sin to others as well as to God. If you have offended someone, the Bible says that first you need to ask that person's forgiveness. In fact, asking the forgiveness of others whom we have offended takes precedence over worshiping God, according to Jesus.

> "If therefore you are presenting your offering at the altar, and there remember that your brother has something against you, leave your offering there before the altar, and go your way; first be reconciled to your brother, and then come and present your offering" (Matt. 5:23-24).

You may also need to make monetary restitution. After conversion Zaccheus, the tax collector, paid back four times the amount of money he stole. If you have cheated someone, you not only need to ask forgiveness but also need to pay him back! Whatever your restitution may involve, it will always mean turning away from known sin. The word *repent* literally means to "have a change of mind" or "to turn around." The word pictures a person heading in one direction, who stops, turns, and goes in an opposite direction.

If you ask God to forgive you, then willingly go out and sin that same sin over and over again, you have not really repented. To truly repent means to turn from sin. I think that is what David had in mind in Psalm 51:16-17: "For Thou dost not delight in sacrifice, otherwise I would give it;/Thou art not pleased with burnt offering./The sacrifices of God are a broken spirit;/A broken and a contrite heart,/O God, Thou wilt not despise." A broken heart—a repentant heart—is one that turns from known sin.

A girl was applying for membership in a church. The deacons were questioning her about her salvation experience.

"Were you a sinner before you trusted Christ?" asked the deacon.

"Yes," replied the girl.

"Do you still sin?" he inquired.

"Yes," she answered.

"Then, what difference has being a Christian made in how you live?"

"I suppose I could explain it this way," said the girl. "Before I was saved, I ran after sin; now I run from it, though it sometimes still overtakes me."

Good answer! A forgiven heart is a changed heart!

What are the consequences of refusing to ask for God's forgiveness? David experienced some of them: depression, loss of spiritual power, and unrelenting feelings of guilt. But Christians who continually refuse to turn from their sins also face the discipline of God. And, as the writer of Hebrews warned: "If we go on sinning willfully after receiving the knowledge of the truth, there no longer remains a sacrifice for sins, but a certain terrifying expectation of judgment" (Heb. 10:26-27).

Ask for God's forgiveness, turn from known sin and begin to experience the freedom of God's forgiveness *today!*

8
Mary
Magnifying the Lord

Several years ago, a television commercial for a certain brand of chili featured a cowboy staring into the camera and asking this penetrating question: "Friend, how long has it been since you've had a big, heaping bowl of [product X] chili? . . . Well, that's *too* long!" Let me change the question just a little: "Friend, how long has it been since you've heard a message on Mary, the mother of Jesus? . . . Well, that's *too* long!"

The fact is that as evangelical Christians we don't hear that much about Mary (with the exception of the obligatory annual Christmas story). Why is that?

I imagine that the doctrinal error of some who overemphasize the place of Mary has caused us to shrink away from examining the life of this remarkable girl. Though some people may believe Mary is a mediator, Protestants believe there is no intermediary between God and man except Jesus Christ: "For there is one God, and one mediator also between God and men, the man Christ Jesus" (1 Tim. 2:5).

Nevertheless, I am afraid we have allowed the error of some to rob us of studying and appreciating the portrait of a girl whom God used significantly. In the story of Mary, we learn something about the kind of person God looks for when He has an important job to accomplish.

A Tale of Two Births

Because of the marriage practices of that day, many people (including myself) believe that Mary was a teenager. To fully appreciate her faith in God, it is helpful to contrast her response to God's message to that of Zacharias.

Luke opens, not with the story of the birth of Christ, but with the story of the birth of John the Baptist to an old couple named Zacharias and Elizabeth.

The Jews had been praying for thousands of years for the Messiah. But before Messiah would come, the Old Testament prophesied the birth of a messenger of the Messiah—someone who would announce His coming. He would be like the mighty prophet Elijah. In fact, the closing words of the Old Testament prophesied about this person: "Behold, I am going to send My messenger, and he will clear the way before Me. . . . Behold, I am going to send you Elijah the prophet before the coming of the great and terrible day of the Lord" (Mal. 3:1; 4:5)

Four hundred years had elapsed, and there was no sign of such a messenger coming, much less a Messiah. Most of the people had given up hope. But suddenly, God began to move. Luke 1 opens with Zacharias, an old man, performing his priestly duties in the Temple. Because there were so many priests, priests served only two weeks a year in the Temple. Lots were cast to determine who would officiate at certain rituals.

By "chance" (see Prov. 16:33: "The lot is cast into the lap, but its every decision is from the Lord") it was Zacharias's turn when God decided to begin to move!

> And an angel of the Lord appeared to him, standing to the right of the altar of incense. And Zacharias was troubled when he saw him, and fear gripped him. But the angel said to him, "Do not be afraid, Zacharias, for your petition has been heard, and your wife Elizabeth will bear you a son, and you will give him the name John . . . And it is he who will go as a forerunner before Him in the spirit and power of Elijah, . . . so as to make ready a people prepared for the Lord" (Luke 1:11-13,17).

Zacharias was busy praying in the Temple. He was praying, no doubt, for the Messiah. Any good priest would be asking for the Deliverer to come and set the people free. But, he was probably also praying for something much more personal—a child for him and his aged wife. Like so many of us, he was surprised when God began to answer his prayers!

Zacharias's initial response was understandable. He was gripped with *phobos* (fear). There are hundreds of phobias today. I read recently of a woman who was fearful of anything associated with the state of Wisconsin! Zacharias and the Jews of his day suffered from "angelphobia." They were afraid of angels! Why? Because angels usually indicated judgment or death. For a man to look on God or on one of His representatives, such as an angel, could have meant certain death. That is why the first words out of Gabriel's mouth were often, "Fear not!"

But Zacharias's continuing disbelief, though human, was displeasing to the Lord. After the announcement, he continued to doubt: "How shall I know this for certain? For I am an old man, and my wife is advanced in years" (Luke 1:18).

Sensing his disbelief, Gabriel pronounced a judgment upon Zacharias: "Behold, you shall be silent and unable to speak until the day when these things take place, because you did not believe my words, which shall be fulfilled in their proper time" (Luke 1:20).

Then the scene shifts to Nazareth. The focus is not on an old man, but on a young woman. In fact, Mary was the opposite of Zacharias in many ways.

Zacharias	Mary
man	woman
old	young
married	single
a priest	a common person

But as we shall see, the most striking contrast between these two lies in their responses to the miraculous message of Gabriel.

We find some information about Mary in Luke 1:26-27: "Now in the sixth month the angel Gabriel was sent from God to a city in Galilee, called Nazareth, to a virgin engaged to a man whose name was Joseph, of the descendants of David; and the virgin's name was Mary."

Notice, first, that she was a virgin—someone who had no previous sexual encounter. She was also engaged. To be engaged then was a much more serious commitment than it is today. In the Jewish culture, an engagement meant oaths had been taken, a dowry had been paid, and the promise of faithfulness had been made. In fact, so serious was this commitment, that if one of the partners were unfaithful, he or she could be put to death (see Deut. 22:23-24). The only difference between an engaged couple and a married couple was the absence of sexual relations.

Mary's first response to Gabriel's message was similar to Zacharias's initial response:

> And coming in, he said to her, "Hail, favored one! The Lord is with you." But she was greatly troubled at this statement, and kept pondering what kind of salutation this might be. And the angel said to her, "Do not be afraid, Mary; for you have found favor with God" (Luke 1:28-30).

The next words of the angel must have boggled Mary's mind. Gabriel's fivefold description of Mary's child was much more exacting than any sonogram!

He will be great. (I agree, that's not too specific. Every mother thinks that—angelic announcement or not!)

He will be called the Son of the Most High. In our culture, we tend to think of the son of a great person as someone with a little less stature than his father. I remember going to see many King Kong and Godzilla movies as a youngster. For some reason, whenever the movie title began with "Son of . . ." we knew we were in for a grade-B picture! But in the Jewish mind, the "son" of someone denoted a carbon copy of the original. Thus, to Mary, this description of her child was the same as saying she would be giving birth to God Himself.

He will be given the throne of David. This was an obvious reference to the messianic prophecy from 2 Samuel 7:16. Mary's son would be the one who fulfilled that prophecy.

He will rule over Israel forever. No one had ever ruled over Israel forever. Struggles from outside forces or strife from within the nation had brought every monarchy in Israel's history to an end. But, the Messiah would be so invincible that no one could ever supplant Him.

His kingdom will have no end. This is not only a reference to the duration of Messiah's rule but also to the scope of His kingdom. His kingdom would include all nations and all of creation.

"Can You Repeat That Again, Slowly?"

Mary's initial response was not unlike that of Zacharias. She asked Gabriel how this could be possible since she was a virgin—a very logical question. "And the angel answered and said to her, 'The Holy Spirit will overshadow you, . . . and for that reason the holy offspring shall be called the Son of God, . . . For nothing will be impossible with God' " (Luke 1:35,37).

But that is where the similarity between Mary and Zacharias ends. Once Gabriel explained that God's power would accomplish this unheard of miracle, Mary expressed her faith in God's ability to perform the act: "And Mary said, "Behold, the bondslave of the Lord; be it done to me according to your word" (Luke 1:38). God had said it, and that settled it for Mary!

Have you ever wondered why God chose Mary to be the mother of the Savior of the world? Of all the billions of women throughout history whom God could have chosen, why did He select this obscure Jewish teenager for this important task? In this story, I believe we can discover at least four principles about the kind of person God uses.

Those Who Are Pure

Notice in Luke 1:27 that Gabriel came to a "virgin." What is the significance of that? Seven hundred years earlier, God had predetermined that the mother of Messiah would be a virgin: "Therefore the Lord Himself will give you a sign: Behold, a virgin will be with child and bear a son, and she will call His name Immanuel" (Isa. 7:14). Don't miss the point here. Even though God had already decided what kind of person this woman had to be (a Jewish virgin from Nazareth), He still had to find someone who met that standard.

Now Mary was no plaster saint. She had the same drives as any healthy girl. Furthermore, she was in love and planning to be married. I imagine that she and Joseph had the same temptations any engaged couple would have. They could have rationalized any sexual involvement by the fact that they would soon be married. So why wait? But had they become sexually involved, Mary would have forfeited her chance to be the one God would use for this mighty miracle.

In my work as a pastor, I counsel many young people who face the same temptation. Several years ago, I came across this article I have given them to read. The headline of the article is "25-year-old Virgin Thinks Waiting Will be Worth It to the Right Man." I have excerpted part of what this girl wrote:

I have yet to fall in love with the man I plan on spending the rest of my life with. That is my one and only prerequisite for sex. I want to be able to share something with him, something truly unique that I have never shared or experienced with anyone else. Archaic? Possibly. And maybe a little too idealistic. After all, chances are he won't be a virgin. But in such transitory times when things can be gotten so easily and just as easily disposed of, I want something to be exclusive . . . At the risk of applying often-used cliches to the issue of sex, I am told patience is a virtue and that good things come those who wait. I hope I find a man someday who will accept this, and I'm positive he won't live to regret it.

Yes, there are some practical, as well as spiritual, benefits to remaining sexually pure.

Some would argue that God is capable of using impure people to carry out His work. "After all, the power is in the message, not in the messenger," they argue. But, given the choice, God will always use a clean vessel instead of a polluted one. That's the point Paul made in 2 Timothy 2:20-21:

> Now in a large house there are not only gold and silver vessels, but also vessels of wood and of earthenware, and some to honor and some to dishonor. Therefore, if a man cleanses himself from these things, he will be a vessel for honor, . . . prepared for every good work.

Let me illustrate the truth of that principle. Suppose you have been outside, working in the heat. You come inside the kitchen, desperate for a drink of water. As you look around for a glass, you see that you only have two choices. One choice is a beautiful crystal goblet that has been sitting in the sink for a week, caked over with film and grime. The other choice is an empty peanut butter jar that has been thoroughly cleaned out, without any residue. Which would you choose to drink from? Obviously, the peanut butter jar! Why? Even though it is not as beautiful as the crystal glass, IT IS CLEAN!

In Mary's day, there may have been girls who were more talented, more beautiful, more flamboyant than Mary, but Mary was pure. And that is God's first requirement to be used by Him.

Those Who Believe His Word

Mary's unwavering faith in God's power was voiced by her relative, Elizabeth. "Blessed is she who believed that there would be a fulfillment of what had been spoken to her by the Lord" (Luke 1:45). The word translated "blessed" literally means "satisfied." Once Mary heard God's message to her, she was satisfied that God would do what He had promised. The writer of Hebrews put it this way: "Without faith it is impossible to please Him, for he who comes to God must believe that He is, and that he is a rewarder of those who seek Him" (Heb. 11:6).

Those Who Place His Glory Above Their Own Reputation

Imagine the ridicule Mary must have endured during the days of her pregnancy. But most of us forget that Mary suffered a bad reputation throughout her entire life. There was a rumor floating around that Mary's baby was the product of an illicit relationship between Mary and a Roman soldier. That rumor was behind the taunt of the Pharisees in John 8:19: "So they were saying to Him, 'Where is Your Father?'" Yet, Mary was willing to suffer the loss of her reputation in exchange for the approval of God.

Are you willing to do that? We don't realize it, but we are hopelessly bound to what others think: If I talk to that person about Christ, what will he think of me? If I say no to this activity, what will my friends think about me? If I were to walk down the aisle of the church and make this decision, what would people say?

All of us want to have the respect of others. We all want to be admired. Nobody likes the label of fanatic. Yet if you are a committed Christian, there will be times that you have to sacrifice the approval of others for God's glory.

How can you handle that rejection? Let me share with you a liberating truth. When people reject you for being God's representative, they aren't rejecting you—they are rejecting God.

How can you be sure that they are rejecting God and not you? By dying! You see, a Christian is one who has died to self. And that means dying to everything one holds important—including one's reputation. That's what Paul had in mind when he wrote, "I have been crucified with Christ; and it is no longer I who live, but Christ lives in me" (Gal.

2:20). Paul did not concern himself with what others thought about him and his preaching. Why? Because Paul was a dead man! And I don't know of any corpses in the cemetery who are concerned about their reputations!

The life of Christ is the supreme example of a "crucified life." Although He was equal to God, He did not hold on to His position. Instead, He "made himself of no reputation, and took upon him the form of a servant, and was made in the likeness of men: And being found in fashion as a man, he humbled himself, and became obedient unto death, even the death of the cross (Phili. 2:7-8, KJV).

Where did Christ learn to subordinate His desires to the will of God? I think it was from His mother, Mary. When she heard God's plan for her life, she simply replied, "Behold, the bondslave of the lord; be it done to me according to your word" (Luke 1:38).

Those Who Are Willing to Sacrifice
That Which Is Most Important to Them

Mary fully realized that by allowing God to use her in this way she was risking her future relationship with Joseph, not to mention her own life! The Old Testament law was clear about the penalty for having a sexual relationship before marriage: "If there is a girl who is a virgin engaged to a man, and another man finds her in the city and lies with her, then you shall bring them both out to the gate of that city and you shall stone them to death" (Deut. 22:23-24).

Mary's pregnancy would have indicated to others that she had violated the above law. When Joseph found out about her situation, he apparently did not want to have her stoned to death—he loved her. Instead, he wanted to end the relationship secretly—no questions asked (Matt. 1:18-19). Think of the heartache this young girl felt as she contemplated the loss of the man she loved. Yet she was willing to give it all up out of obedience to God.

To be a disciple of Christ requires that we be willing to give up everything for Him—money, relationships, reputation, and even life. Mary was willing to do this. Are you?

Jim Elliot was a young man who totally surrendered his life to God. Ultimately that involved his brutal murder by the Auca Indians, as he and four others tried to share the gospel with those natives. When he was twenty-two years of age and a student at Wheaton College, Elliot wrote these words in his journal: "He is no fool who gives up what he cannot keep in order to gain what he cannot lose." Those are words to remember when following Christ seems too costly.

9
Peter
Climbing Off the Spiritual Roller Coaster

Several years ago I was traveling to another city. On the plane, I read an article in the in-flight magazine about the ten fastest roller coasters in the United States. Since one of them was in the city I was traveling to, and since I am a sucker for a good roller coaster ride, I decided to stop by the amusement park on the way into town (Yes, I realize this was not a very "ministerial" thing to do, but it was GREAT fun!).

I soon found myself standing in line for the ride, dressed in my ministerial garb (suit, tie, color-coordinated pocket square) along with several thousand more appropriately dressed tourists. It was the middle of the summer, and I was drenched with perspiration by the time I finally reached my turn in the thrill machine.

The coaster slowly, but deliberately, made its way up the incline. Then . . . SWOOSH . . . we were off! Up . . . down . . . around . . . and, yes, even upside down. Going at speeds up to sixty miles per hour! Within a few minutes, we were back where we started. As I was climbing out of my seat, I was struck with the irony of the experience. I had spent several hours in line for a ride that was over in a few minutes, and I had not gone anywhere. Sure, it was thrilling at moments, but no progress had been made.

Many peoples' spiritual lives are like that—many highs and lows, but not much progress. Why? Anytime your faith is based on your emotions, you will find yourself, as a popular song goes, being "up, down, trying to get that feeling again."

While that kind of Christianity may have its moments of exhilaration, I'm convinced that God never meant for us to live like that. Instead, He desires for us to be consistent in our relationship to Him. How do you remain steady in your Christian walk? A look at the experience of Peter provides the answers. No character in the New Testament ran hotter or colder in the Christian life than Peter. Yet, at the crossroads of his spiritual life, he found the keys of consistency that transformed him into a mighty servant of God.

Snapshots from Peter's Life

When studying the Gospels, we need to remember that these accounts are not complete records of everything Jesus and His disciples said and did. Instead, the Gospels record the significant events that God wanted us to know.

In many ways, the Gospels are like a photograph album. If I were to ask you what has happened in your family during the last ten years, it would be impossible for you to tell everything that had occurred. Instead, you might pull out a picture album showing the momentous events in your family's life—graduations, weddings, and holidays.

To fully appreciate the dramatic transformation of Peter, it would be helpful for us to look at some "snapshots" of his life. What you will see in each of these examples is that there was not much time between the highs and the lows in Peter's spiritual life.

Don't Swim After a Heavy Meal

The first example of Peter's volatility I want you to notice is found in Matthew 14. Jesus had spent the day healing the multitudes. Evening was coming, and the disciples were starting to think about their dinner plans. Not wanting to have to pick up the supper tab for the five thousand people, the disciples suggested that Jesus pronounce a quick benediction and send the people into town to fend for themselves.

But Jesus had a different idea.

Jesus said to them, "They do not need to go away; you give them something to eat!" And they said to Him, "We have here only five loaves and two fish." And He said, "Bring them here to Me." And ordering the multitudes to recline on the grass, he took the five loaves and the two fish, and looking up toward heaven, He blessed the food, and breaking the loaves He gave them to the disciples, and the disciples gave to the multitudes, and they all ate, and were satisfied. And they picked up what was left over of the broken pieces, twelve full baskets.

And there were about five thousand men who ate, aside from women and children (Matt. 14:16-21).

Peter had just witnessed a demonstration of the power of Christ. Imagine! Thousands of people fed with only five loaves of bread, two fish!

Notice what happened next. Jesus sent the disciples in a boat across the Sea of Galilee. He appeared to them, walking on the water:

> But immediately Jesus spoke to them, saying, "Take courage, it is I; do not be afraid." And Peter answered Him and said, "Lord, if it is You, command me to come to You on the water." And he said, "Come!" And Peter got out of the boat, and walked on the water and came toward Jesus. But seeing the wind, he became afraid, and beginning to sink, he cried out saying, "Lord, save me!" (Matt. 14:27-30).

Jesus had just demonstrated His power to the disciples through the feeding of the five thousand. Now, Jesus decided to give them a test to see if they understood who He was. Unfortunately, they received an *F* (and that wasn't for "faith" either!).

No doubt Peter had a feeling of ecstasy after the feeding of the five thousand men. It proved he was following the right guy after all. I imagine he was proud to be one of the inner circle of the Messiah. But in a matter of hours, Peter had sunk (pardon the pun) to a spiritual low. Why?

One small phrase gives us the answer: "Seeing the wind, he became afraid." Peter took his eyes off Christ and started noticing his dire circumstances—out on a stormy sea with no visible means of support! Whenever people start looking at circumstances instead of the Lord who controls circumstances, they are destined to become discouraged.

I think about the apostle Paul as he wrote to the church at Philippi. Remember some of the things he said?

> "Rejoice in the Lord always; again I will say, rejoice!" (4:4).

> "Be anxious for nothing, but in everything by prayer and supplication with thanksgiving let your requests be made known to God" (4:6).

> "I have learned to be content in whatever circumstances I am" (4:11).

> "I can do all things through Him who strengthens me" (4:13).

Don't write Paul's words off as empty optimism until you understand his situation. He was not on the French Riviera, sipping a cool drink, as he penned these words. He was imprisoned in Rome, facing his possible execution. Yet, Paul testified he had learned the "secret of being filled and going hungry, both of having abundance and suffering need" (v. 12).

What is that secret? It's learning to quit pinning your hopes on the uncertainty of circumstances. Someone has said that the basis of all insecurity is trusting in something that can be taken away. If your happiness is dependent on a person, you will be happy until that person is taken away. If your joy is based on your job, you will be content until your job changes. If your satisfaction is based on money, you will be fulfilled until you lose it.

But if your joy is based on Christ, you can have the same optimism that Paul had. Evangelist D. L. Moody put it like this: "Trust in yourself, and you are doomed to disappointment; trust in your friends and, they will die or leave you; trust in money, and it may be taken away from you, but trust in God, and you are never to be confounded in time or eternity."

Between a Rock and a Hard Place

Another example of Peter's inconsistency is seen in Matthew 16. Jesus conducted a poll among His disciples concerning His identity. Public opinion was mixed, they said. But Jesus was more interested in who the disciples thought He was: " 'But who do you say that I am?' And Simon Peter answered and said, 'Thou art the Christ, the Son of the living God'." (Matt. 16:16).

I can just see Jesus asking that question. Peter wasn't the brightest guy around, but he knew the right answer. Can't you just see him in schoolboy eagerness raising his hand, straining to get the Teacher's attention?

"I know, I know the answer, Jesus!"

"All right, Peter, tell us."

"Thou art the Christ, the Son of the Living God." I can picture Peter beaming with pride, as the other disciples roll their eyes.

Notice the way Jesus brags on Peter: "Blessed are you, Simon Barjona, because flesh and blood did not reveal this to you, but My Father who is in heaven. And I also say to you that you are Peter, and upon this rock I will build My church; and the gates of Hades shall not overpower it" (Matt. 16:17-18).

What was Jesus saying to Peter? A look at the original text unravels the difficulty of this verse. The name Peter *(petros)* means "rock" or "rock-man." But Jesus used the feminine form of "rock" *(petra)* in referring to the foundation of the church. Thus, the "rock" Jesus was referring to was not Peter, but Peter's statement of Jesus' identity. The church is not built on Peter, but on the truth of Peter's confession: Jesus Christ is the Son of God.

Nevertheless, Peter *had* articulated the very basis of the Christian faith. No doubt this was the high water mark in Peter's spiritual life. But notice, again, what happened immediately after that experience: "From that time Jesus Christ began to show His disciples that he must go to Jerusalem, and suffer many things from the elders and chief priests and scribes, and be killed, and be raised up on the third day" (Matt. 16:21-22).

Now Peter was no Phi Beta Kappa, but he immediately understood the implication of what Jesus was saying. If Jesus were to be put to death, His disciples were likely to be in big trouble too. And at this stage in his spiritual life, Peter was not keen on the idea of suffering. So he tried to talk Jesus out of this course of action: "And Peter took Him aside and began to rebuke Him, saying, 'God forbid it, Lord! This shall never happen to You.' But He turned and said to Peter, 'Get behind Me, Satan! You are a stumbling block to Me; for you are not setting your mind on God's interests, but man's' " (Matt. 16:22-23).

One moment Jesus was praising Peter for his strong faith; the next moment, Jesus was rebuking him for being the mouthpiece of Satan.

Wherever He Leads I'll Go . . . Maybe

I want us to look at just one more snapshot of Peter's life. It's found in Mark 14. It was the night before Jesus' death. He had gathered His disciples together for a meal and an explanation of what was about to take place. After the meal, they started walking together, and Jesus made a prediction about them: "You will all fall away, because it is written, 'I will strike down the shepherd, and the sheep shall be scattered' " (v. 27).

But Peter could not accept such an idea. " 'Even though all may fall away, yet I will not.' And Jesus said to him, 'Truly I say to you, that you yourself this very night, before a cock crows twice, shall three times deny Me.' But Peter kept saying insistently, 'Even if I have to die with You, I will not deny You!' " (vv. 29-31). I believe that Peter really meant that . . . for the moment. But within a few hours, he was denying Christ.

Later that same evening, Jesus was taken for a hearing before the high priest, Caiaphas, and the Sanhedrin. It wasn't looking good for Jesus.

> As Peter was below in the courtyard, one of the servant-girls of the high priest came, and seeing Peter warming himself, she looked at him, and said, "You, too, were with Jesus the Nazarene." But he denied it, saying, "I neither know nor understand what you are talking about." And he went out onto the porch. And the maid saw him, and began once more to say to the bystanders, "This is one of them!" But again he was denying it. And after a while the bystanders were again saying to Peter, "Surely you are one of them, for you are a Galilean too." But he began to curse and swear, "I do not know this fellow you are talking about!" And immediately a cock crowed a second time. And Peter remembered how Jesus had made the remark to him, "Before a cock crows twice, you will deny Me three times." And he began to weep [lit. "he wept continually, bitterly"] (Mark 14:66-72).

What caused this outburst of bitter crying? Maybe he was despondent over the fact that the cause to which he had devoted himself seemed to be coming to an abrupt end. But more likely, he finally had an accurate picture of himself. He was no "rock." His faith was steadfast only as long as the circumstances were favorable. He was a disappointment to himself and to the Lord who had believed in him.

A Second Chance

But Jesus was not through with Peter. The next picture of Peter we see is in John 21. Jesus had risen from the grave, just as He had promised. Meanwhile, Peter was back at his old trade—fishing for fish instead of for men. In a scene reminiscent of the first time the disciples were called, the risen Lord appeared to them and gave them some fishing tips.

When Peter realized it was the Lord, he was filled with excitement! "And so when Simon Peter heard that it was the Lord, he put his outer garment on (for he was stripped for work), and threw himself into the sea" (John 21:7).

Jesus was ready to give Peter another chance to prove his loyalty. In a setting similar to the one in which Peter denied Christ (by a charcoal fire), Christ asked him, "Do you love me?" And three times, Peter had an opportunity to affirm his devotion to Christ.

But it was still a conditional devotion. As soon as Christ prophesied that Peter would die a martyr's death, Jesus commanded, "Follow Me!" (John 21:19). But before Peter followed Him, he wanted to know what was going to happen to the rest of the disciples, especially John: "Peter, turning around, saw the disciple whom Jesus loved following them; . . . [and] said to Jesus, 'Lord, and what about this man?' Jesus said to him, 'If I want him to remain until I come, what is that to you? You follow me!' (21:20-22). Peter's faith was still tied to circumstances. But Jesus gave Peter the solution to his instability: Quit worrying about circumstances and other people and follow Me.

I think that truth is what the writer of Hebrews had in mind when he wrote, "Let us run with endurance the race that is set before us, fixing our eyes on Jesus, the author and perfecter of faith" (12:1-2). A runner who keeps looking at other runners is destined to stumble. A driver who only gazes at other motorists is destined to crash. In the same way, a Christian who focuses on other people, and how God chooses to deal with them, will fall.

Peter—the Rock

As we turn a few pages in the "photo album" to Acts 2, we see a completely different Peter. It is hard to recognize him in this "picture." He doesn't appear to be the same person we have seen before. Instead, he is courageous and unwavering in his faith. Before a crowd of thousands, many of whom were responsible for the crucifixion of Christ a few weeks earlier, he takes his stand with Christ.

> But Peter, taking his stand with the eleven, raised his voice and declared to them: "Men of Judea, and all you who live in Jerusalem, let this be known to you, and give heed to my words. . . . Jesus the Nazarene, a man attested to you by God with miracles and wonders and signs which God performed through Him in your midst, just as you yourselves know—this Man, delivered up by the predetermined plan

and foreknowledge of God, you nailed to a cross by the hands of godless men and put Him to death" (vv. 14, 22-24).

Talk about bold! Peter was talking to a group that would just as soon crucify *him* as listen to him! What had transformed Peter into such a courageous and consistent follower of Christ? I think Peter finally learned three principles about consistency in the Christian life that became the bedrock of his faith. What are they?

The Peter Principles

Consistency Comes from Obedience, Not Feeling

When the Lord asked Peter if he loved Him, Peter was quick with all kinds of superlatives about his love for Jesus. But Jesus said that love for Him had to be translated into obedience ("Feed My sheep," and "Follow Me"). That is what Jesus had always taught His disciples: "If you love me, you will keep My commandments" (John 14:15).

How different that is from our mind-set today. We live in a feeling-oriented society: "If it feels good do it "(and the corollary, "if it doesn't feel good, don't do it!). That kind of attitude creates inconsistency in every part of our lives.

A husband or wife seeks a divorce because he or she "doesn't feel anything any longer." People quit their jobs because they "don't feel fulfilled." Christians quit going to church because they "don't feel the Spirit in the services."

But God's Word teaches that right actions produce right feelings—not vice versa. Don't wait until you "feel right" to "do right"; do right, and then you will feel right!

A verse in the Old Testament affirms this truth. It is found in Genesis 4. Cain was despondent because his brother, Abel, had offered an acceptable sacrifice to God, and Cain's gift had been rejected. Look at what the Lord said about Cain's depression: "Then the Lord said to Cain, 'Why are you angry? And why has your countenance fallen? If you do well, will not your countenance be lifted up? And if you do not do well, sin is couching at the door; and its desire is for you, but you must master it' " (vv. 6-7).

I can't tell you the number of people who have said to me, "Robert, I feel so blah about my Christianity." When I ask them about their spiritual disciplines—reading God's Word, praying, and witnessing—they reply, "I just don't feel like it." I always have the same reply, "If you wait until you feel like it, you'll never do it. Do it out of obedience, and then you will start feeling like it."

Consistency Is Based on
Understanding Our Relationship to Christ

For a long time, Peter felt that Jesus' love for him was based on his performance. Yet, over a period of years Peter saw that, in spite of his mammoth failures, Christ still loved him. Isn't it interesting that after Peter had so blatantly denied knowing Christ, Jesus still chose to appear to him first, after His resurrection?

I think that the assurance of Christ's unwavering love gave Peter the motivation for his Christian service. Something about knowing that a person loves you unconditionally motivates you to want to do as much as you can for that person.

Consistency Based on
the Foundation of God's Word

It's no accident that Jesus told Peter three times to "feed My sheep." Peter's entire ministry was to be centered around proclaiming the truth of God's Word. That's why Peter wrote that the key to Christian growth was a regular intake of the Word of God: "Like newborn babes, long for the pure milk of the word, that by it you may grow in respect to salvation" (1 Peter 2:2).

Peter was not void of any emotion in his faith. But as a follower of Christ, and as a leader in the church, Peter had come to see that God's Word, not human emotions, was the only stable foundation on which to build one's life.

I think one of the most amazing testimonies to the importance of Scripture was penned by Peter:

> For we did not follow cleverly devised tales when we made known to you the power and coming of our Lord Jesus Christ, but we were eyewitnesses of His majesty. . . . and we ourselves heard this utterance made from heaven when we were with Him on the holy mountain. And so we have the prophetic word made more sure, to which you do well to pay attention as to a lamp shining in a dark place (2 Pet. 1:16-18).

Did you catch what Peter was saying? Even though he was an eyewitness to the work of Christ, even though he had seen His majesty revealed at the transfiguration, Peter also had a basis for his faith in the Word of God!

An old pastor had been forced to retire. His voice cracked from years of preaching. One day he was invited by a friend to an elegant luncheon. Although he was out of his league, he went. The guest speaker at the luncheon was a famous actor. Someone asked the actor if he would do a dramatic reading. He responded by saying that he had an endless repertoire and would take a request. The old pastor said, "How about the Twenty-third Psalm." The actor responded, "That's a little unusual; but, since I know it, I will do it on one condition. You must do it after I do it." Though embarrassed, the pastor agreed.

The great actor recited the passage with resonant intonation, a beautiful, lyrical voice, and tremendous interpretation. When he finished, there was thunderous applause. The old pastor stood up and, with a breaking voice, simply recited the passage as he had so many times before. When he was finished, there was not a dry eye in the room. Sensing the emotion of the moment, the actor stood up and declared, "I think I understand the difference in your response to me and to the pastor. I know the psalm, but he knows the Shepherd!"

Peter knew the Shepherd. And he finally discovered that the key to consistency in his commitment to the Shepherd was an unconditional obedience to the Shepherd's Word.

10
Mary and Martha
Serving in Different Ways

Luke's Gospel relates the story of Mary's and Martha's approach to serving Jesus in five *short* verses. I have examined this passage closely, and I see a basic truth that, if properly understood, would solve a lot of conflicts among Christians.

Guess Who's Coming to Dinner?

The home of Lazarus was one of Jesus' favorite places to visit. For some reason, the Master had a special affection for Lazarus and his two sisters, Mary and Martha. They lived in Bethany, a village a few miles east of Jerusalem. Jesus chose to spend the last week of his life with them.

On one of His visits to Jerusalem, Jesus dropped in at this home for a visit.

> Now as they were traveling along, He entered a certain village; and a woman named Martha welcomed Him into her home. And she had a sister called Mary, who moreover was listening to the Lord's word, seated at His feet. But Martha was distracted with all her preparations; and she came up to him, and said, "Lord, do You not care that my sister has left me to do all the serving alone? Then tell her to help me." But the Lord answered and said to her, "Martha, Martha, you are worried and bothered about so many things; but only a few things are necessary, really only one, for Mary has chosen the good part, which shall not be taken away from her" (Luke 10:38-42).

A careful examination of the story reveals that this was not a case of one sister's being excited about Jesus' visit and the other's not caring. Martha was just as excited over His visit as her sister. In fact, she was the first one at the door to welcome Jesus. And her enthusiasm continued as she scurried about trying to get everything ready for the meal.

On the other hand, Mary seated herself at Jesus' feet. She was intent on listening to every word the Lord uttered. She had the proper reverence for Jesus, as revealed by her position at his feet.

The text says that Martha was "distracted with all her preparations." She, like many of us on occasion, was overly concerned with caring for her special guest. I don't want to make the mistake that some do of coming down too hard on Martha. Some commentaries give the impression that Mary was performing the holy task while Martha cared nothing about being with Jesus.

No, Martha was performing an important task—serving. Someone had to prepare the meal! But her focus was off. She became so wrapped up in her service that she lost sight of the objective—fellowship with the Lord. From her point of view, we can easily understand why she blew her stack when she saw her sister just sitting. Martha asked the Lord to make Mary get up and help serve the meal.

Jesus compassionately (notice the repetition of her name: "Martha, Martha") tried to redirect her priorities. This was not a harsh condemnation of her service. He realized that she wanted the meal to be lovely, out of devotion to Him. But He desired to relieve her of the pressure she felt from the burden of details and to redirect her attention to Him. In the end, He reminded her, there was only one thing that was important—fellowship with God.

I read the story of a man who had lost his wife. They had had one daughter, and the father loved to be with her. When he came home from work, they ate dinner together and then had several hours to visit, to read aloud together, or to sing. He found deep comfort in the company of his daughter. As the end of the year approached, the girl said to her father one evening, "Please excuse me; I have something I need to do in my room." The next night she said the same thing. Night after night she made the same excuse, much to his disappointment. But he never asked what she was doing. Finally, Christmas morning arrived. She came into her father's room and said, "Merry Christmas, Dad!" She handed him a pair of crocheted slippers which she had spent the evenings making for him. He said after he thanked her, "These are beautiful, but I would much rather have had you with me all those lonely evenings than to have these slippers, beautiful and comfortable as they are."

I think that is what the Lord was saying to Martha and to all of us. He appreciates our service; but, above all, He desires our fellowship.

Two Sisters—Two Personalities

Only a superficial reading of this story would cause one to see the contrast between Mary and Martha as that of light to darkness. Too often Martha has been criticized as the worldly-minded and jealous half of the pair while Mary was the more spiritually minded one. An examination of Martha's life reveals that she had many positive qualities.

First, she was hospitable. The fact that she was the first one to greet Jesus indicates that she may have been the owner of the house. And it was always open to the Lord. Martha was always excited to see Jesus. Later, when Jesus came to raise Lazarus from the dead, Martha greeted Him first: "Martha, therefore, when she heard that Jesus was coming, went to meet Him; but Mary still sat in the house" (John 11:20).

You can be sure that whenever Jesus visited He lacked for nothing. I am confident that she was the kind of hostess who never needed to apologize for a messy house or an empty refrigerator. She was the consumate hostess! Eugenia Price wrote this about Martha's hospitality:

> The superb hospitality He found in Martha's home was extremely important to Him. No one enjoyed her cooking more than He enjoyed it. No one found her spacious home more beautiful, more inviting. But always He had the real issues in full view. He could not be distracted from them, even by His tired body and His human need of Martha's services.[1]

Second, she was a woman of deep faith. The care she took in preparation for the Lord's visit testified of her faith in Jesus as the Messiah. This faith was later revealed in the raising of her brother, Lazarus, from the dead.

> Martha therefore said to Jesus, "Lord, if You had been here, my brother would not have died. Even now I know that whatever You ask

of God, God will give You." Jesus said to her, "Your brother shall rise again." Martha said to Him, "I know that he will rise again in the resurrection on the last day." Jesus said to her, "I am the resurrection and the life; he who believes in Me shall live even if he dies and everyone who lives and believes in Me shall never die. Do you believe this?" She said to Him, "Yes, Lord; I have believed that You are the Christ, the Son of God, even He who comes into the world" (John 11:21-26).

Third, she was loved by the Lord. John's Gospel tells us that Jesus loved Martha, Mary, and Lazarus. The Lord loved Martha just as much as Mary. He had created both of them and had given them unique personalities.

Mary—Learning to Listen to God

We also do an injustice to the story if we simply paint Mary as a lazy woman, content to let someone else do the work. Let's not forget that the Lord commended Mary for having the right priorities. Mary knew the importance of listening to the Lord. She also had learned the secrets of *how* to listen to the Lord. Mary demonstrated that listening to God involves . . .

Being in the Right Position Before God

Mary was seated at Jesus' feet (Luke 10:39). She realized who He was and, as a result, felt that she should kneel at His feet. Her reverence for the Lord is demonstrated by a later act recorded in John 12. Jesus had dropped in for another visit, sometime after He had raised Lazarus from the dead. Martha was busy serving, and Lazarus was reclining at the table, listening to the Master. "Mary therefore took a pound of very costly, genuine spikenard ointment, and anointed the feet of Jesus, and wiped His feet with her hair; and the house was filled with the fragrance" (v. 3).

Some started to question Mary's apparent waste. After all, Judas Iscariot argued, that perfume cost three hundred denarii—almost a year's wages. But, Jesus commended her for her worshipful attitude, again demonstrated by her kneeling at Jesus' feet.

Why am I making such a big deal about Mary's kneeling? Because it indicates her awareness of her spiritual position before God. She understood that she was a sinner in need of a Savior. That attitude is crucial to hearing God's voice. God does not speak to those who have not been forgiven. The psalmist said it this way: "If I regard wickedness in my heart, The Lord will not hear" (66:18).

A person who refuses to kneel before God is someone who doesn't understand the need to be forgiven. I think of the story of the Pharisee and the tax-gatherer, recorded in Luke 18:10-14. The Pharisee stood, with his eyes lifted toward heaven, and thanked God that he was not a sinner like others. The tax-gatherer, realizing his sinfulness, refused to raise his eyes to heaven, and simply prayed, "God, be merciful to me, the sinner!" Jesus said that only the latter was forgiven. And, therefore, he was the only one who could enjoy a relationship with God.

Developing the Right Priorities

Martha fell into the same trap into which many of us fall. She allowed good things to distract her from the best thing. Many of us get so caught up in the urgency of things that need to be done NOW that we keep putting off things that don't cry out for attention, such as fellowship with God. "Maybe I'll have time tomorrow for my quiet time with God—I have too much to do today." We live under the "tyranny of the urgent." Dwight D. Eisenhower said, "I have come to learn that urgent things are seldom important, and the important things are seldom urgent."

On the other hand, Mary understood that spending time with the Lord and listening to His words were so important that everything else would have to take second place. Brother Lawrence expressed that truth in his book *The Practice of the Presence of God:*

> The most holy practice, the nearest to daily life, and the most essential for the spiritual life, is the practice of the presence of God, that is to find joy in his divine company and to make it a habit of life, speaking humbly and conversing lovingly with him at all times, every moment, without rule or restriction, above all at times of temptation, distress, dryness, and revulsion, and even of faithlessness and sin.

Focusing on the Right Person

My three-month-old daughter, Julia, loves to eat! Feeding times are the highlights of her day. She concentrates on her bottle intently— until someone comes into the room or the television is turned on or the telephone rings. Then she forgets all about the bottle. It's not because she isn't hungry. But she is easily distracted. That is characteristic of an infant.

Distraction was also Martha's problem. She eagerly anticipated Jesus' company. But, as Luke said, she "was distracted with all her preparations." Then, her attention shifted from her preparations to her sister. She was worried that Mary was not doing her part.

The Lord, discerning her problem, observed, "Martha, Martha, you are worried and bothered *about so many things*" [emphasis mine]. That was the crux of Martha's problem—she focused on everything except the Lord. And the result was that she was stressed out!

Almost every emotional problem I deal with as a pastor—bitterness, depression, anger, and worry—stems from people shifting their focus away from God to other people or circumstances. The result is that they are spiritually blocked from hearing the voice of God. That is why the writer of Hebrews said that the only way we could live the Christian life successfully was by "fixing our eyes on Jesus, the author and perfecter of faith" (Heb. 12:2).

"Vive' La Difference!"

This story was not intended to exalt Mary and to denounce Martha. Both sisters had strengths and corresponding weaknesses. Someone has said that a character weakness is simply a strength misused. Martha had a desire to meet the temporal needs of her guest—the weakness was that she neglected her own spiritual need. On the other hand, Mary wanted to hear the words of the Lord, but she forgot to give the practical assistance her sister needed.

I see the same truth in the church today. Different Christians have different ways of serving Christ. Or, as the Bible says, we each have a different spiritual gift. I am convinced that understanding the concept of spiritual gifts would settle most conflicts in churches today. I think it would have helped Mary and Martha understand themselves, and one another, more fully. Let me point out some basic truths about spiritual gifts.

Every Christian Has a Spiritual Gift

When you were born into the world, you were born with certain natural abilities. Some of you were born with the gift of music, some with the gift of speaking, some with the gift of working with your hands. In the same way, when you were born *again* into the family of God, you were given a certain spiritual gift in order to be able to function effectively in the body of Christ on earth—the church. In Romans 12:4-6, Paul wrote:

> For just as we have many members in one body and all the members do not have the same function, so we, who are many, are one body in Christ, and individually members one of another. And since we have gifts that differ according to the grace given to us, let each exercise them accordingly: if prophecy, according to the proportion of his faith: if service, in his serving; or he who teaches, in his teaching; or he who exhorts, in his exhortation; he who gives, with liberality; he who leads, with diligence; he who shows mercy, with cheerfulness.

A spiritual gift can be defined as the *desire and the power God gives you to express the message of Christ to others.* For some, like Martha, that motivation will be through serving. For others, it will be through showing mercy to others; and for still others it might be through teaching (I think this might have been Mary's gift, since she was so intent on hearing the words of Christ). A spiritual gift is not only a certain desire that God gives us to do His will but also a certain enabling power He gives us through the Holy Spirit.

Now, let me be quick to say, the Bible commands every Christian to do all of the things listed in Romans 12: prophesy, serve, teach, exhort, give, lead, and show mercy. But there is a certain gift that God has given you that will be not only your basic motivation to serve Him but also an area in your life that God blesses in an unusual and powerful way.

Notice, too, that Scripture indicates that only one gift, from the list in Romans 12, is given to every Christian. In 1 Peter 4:10, the word *gift* is singular in form: "As each one has received a special gift, employ it in serving one another, as good stewards of the manifold grace of God."

Although there are a variety of ministries (also referred to as "gifts" by some people) through which a person might exercise his or her gift, there is only one basic motivation that God has given the individual to use in accomplishing His eternal purpose.

Excitement Comes from Exercising Our Spiritual Gift

All of us have a desire to be a part of something meaningful in life. Very few people in today's society want any more meaningless activities. But, people are begging for meaningful tasks in which to be involved. And what could be a more meaningful activity than participating in the eternal plan of the Creator of the universe! God has chosen to carry out that plan through the local church. Only through the proper use of spiritual gifts can the local church function properly. Thus, if you want to be a part of God's exciting program, you must know and use your spiritual gift!

It is no accident that the word translated "gift" in Romans 12 is the Greek word *charismaton*. What is fascinating about the word is that it comes from the root word *char*, which means "joy," and *charis*, which means "grace." There is an inseparable link among spiritual gifts, joy, and grace. When we accept the grace of the Lord Jesus Christ, the Holy Spirit comes to reside in us and brings with Him a particular enabling gift to assist us in carrying out His purpose. When we exercise that gift, we find true joy and meaning in our life.

Each Gift Is Designed to Perfect the Body of Christ

If only Mary and Martha had understood this truth! No one Christian has all of the gifts. Why? God wants us to learn to cooperate. So, He has given each one of us a valuable gift that will not only be used to minister to unbelievers but will also be used to make each of us more like the Christ. No Christian was designed to operate in isolation. That is why Paul compared the body of Christ, the church, to the human body:

> For even as the body is one and yet has many members, and all the members of the body, though they are many, are one body, so also is Christ. But now God has placed the members, each one of them, in the body, just as he desired. And if they were all one member, where would the body be? And the eye cannot say to the hand, "I have no need of you"; or again the head to the feet, "I have no need of you." Now you are Christ's body and individually members of it (1 Cor. 12:12, 18-19, 21, 27).

What could be a better picture of cooperation than the human body? Think about it. Your stomach gets hungry; your eyes spot a hamburger; your hands grab the burger, douse it with mustard, and shove it into your mouth; and it goes to your stomach. Now, that's cooperation! Paul said that is how the church is supposed to function. Each of us is important in the body of Christ. We do not all have the same gifts, but each gift is vitally important to the healthy functioning of the church.

How does the exercising of spiritual gifts help perfect the body of Christ? Let's take Mary and Martha. Martha's gift was serving—the desire to express the message of Christ by meeting the practical needs of others. On the other hand, Mary's gift may have been teaching or prophecy since she was so interested in the words of Christ. Obviously, since Martha's gift was serving, she reacted to Mary because she was not serving. God wanted Mary to learn the importance of serving that is part of a Christlike character. So, He used Martha, someone with the gift of serving, to point out that "blind spot" in Mary's life.

On the other hand, Mary's exercising her gift would be a motivation for Martha to learn the importance of listening to God. Proverbs 27:17 states, "Iron sharpens iron,/So one man sharpens another." God's purpose in giving us unique spiritual gifts was to make us dependent on one another for the development of a Christlike character.

It is always fascinating to me how knowing a person's spiritual gift helps me to anticipate what his or her response to a situation will be. Years ago, as I was conducting a Sunday School teachers' meeting, I told our teachers that they needed to add more application to the content they were teaching.

During the time I was making this presentation on the importance of application in teaching, I could see several people on the back row who had the spiritual gift of teaching starting to react violently to what I was saying. Those with the spiritual gift of teaching tend to place a heavy emphasis on the presentation of content, instead of the application of that content.

However, those in the group who had the gift of exhortation—giving specific insights to individuals about their individual problems—were applauding what I was saying. Those with the gift of mercy (like my wife!) were afraid that I had hurt the feelings of those with the gift of teaching. And those with the gift of serving were too busy getting the refreshments ready to care about what was being said!

And yet, even before I started my presentation, I was able to anticipate all of those responses because I knew the spiritual gifts of each of those personalities. All of those people had important insights to offer. We do need people with the gifts of teaching to keep us doctrinally sound, just as we need those with the gifts of serving, mercy, and exhortation.

I am convinced that Martha and Mary would have profited from understanding that God had given them a unique gift and, therefore, a unique perspective.

Why did God give different spiritual gifts to different Christians? So we could learn to depend on one another. No Christian was designed to operate in isolation. The legendary football coach, Vince Lombardi, was once asked about his formula for success. He replied, "If you're going to play together as a team, you've got to care for one another. You've got to love each other. Each player has to be thinking about the next guy and saying to himself: 'If I don't block that man, Paul [Hornung] is going to get his legs broken. I have to do my job well in order that he can do his.' The difference between mediocrity and greatness is the feeling these guys have for each other. Most people call it team spirit. When the players are imbued with that special feeling, you know you've got yourself a winning team."

Each player thinking about the next guy, doing his job well so that others can do their job well—that is not only the formula for a winning football team but also for a winning church!

***If you would like a more detailed explanation about how you can discover what your spiritual gift is, let me recommend my three-part video series, "Discovering Your Spiritual Gift."

11
Paul
Capitalizing on One's Handicaps

A man was being honored as his city's leading citizen. At the ceremony, he was asked to tell the story of his life. "Neighbors, when I first came to this town twenty-five years ago, I walked down this dirt road with only the suit on my back, the shoes on my feet, and everything I owned wrapped in a red bandana tied to a stick. Today, I own office buildings, hotel complexes, banks, and I am on the board of thirty-seven leading corporations. This city has been good to me." After the dinner, an eager boy approached the man and asked, "Mister, would you mind telling me what you had wrapped in that red bandana?" "Son," he replied, "I believe it was about $500,000 in cash and $800,000 in government bonds!"

The Declaration of Independence says that all men are equal before the law. However, we know that each of us enters this world with different opportunities and limitations. I believe that the secret of successful living is to recognize and utilize both the gifts *and* the handicaps that God has given us. Yes, you read it correctly! God gives us gifts and handicaps to accomplish His purpose for our lives.

In the chapter on Mary and Martha, we looked at the different gifts God gives Christians. In this chapter, we are going to talk about handicaps. A look at the life of the apostle Paul provides a perfect model for dealing with handicaps in life.

Looks Can Be Deceiving

"He's the greatest preacher since the apostle Paul!" A person who says that may think he's paying the preacher a great compliment. But, in reality, it is an insult! The fact is that Paul wasn't any gifted orator. In 2 Corinthians 10:10 Paul recorded others' observations about his preaching: "For they say, 'His letters are weighty and strong, but his personal presence is unimpressive, and his speech contemptible.' "

Obviously, he wasn't much to look at, either. The above verse, coupled with some of the apocryphal accounts of Paul's life, paints a picture of a man who had been repeatedly beaten with the ugly stick! Look at this account from the apocryphal *Acts of Paul and Thecla:* "And he saw Paul coming, a man little of stature, thin-haired upon the head, crooked in the legs, of good state of body, with eyebrows joining, and nose somewhat hooked."

Part of Paul's problem may have been the "thorn in the flesh" he referred to in 2 Corinthians 12. While some commentators try to spiritualize this handicap, most agree that it was some physical infirmity.

> "The best commentators are, with reason, agreed that the word *skolopos* (thorn) must be taken in the natural sense, as denoting some very painful disorder or mortifying infirmity; . . . a most probable conjecture is that it was a *paralytic* and *hypochondriac affection,* which occasioned a distortion of countenance, and many other distressing effects, which would much tend to impair his usefulness."[1]

This affliction may have contributed to Paul's trembling described in 1 Corinthians 2:3: "And I was with you in weakness and in fear and in much trembling." In spite of these obstacles, Paul did more to spread the gospel of Jesus Christ around the world than any man in history. How? By learning to capitalize on his handicaps.

I believe that Paul's crossroads experience is recorded in 2 Corinthians 12. Up to that point in his ministry, Paul may have believed that his physical impairment was only temporary. Maybe he thought God would remove his affliction so that he could be of greater service. But, finally, Paul began to see the bigger picture concerning his handicap:

> Because of the surpassing greatness of the revelations, for this reason, to keep me from exalting myself, there was given me a thorn in the flesh, a messenger of Satan to buffet me—to keep me from exalting myself! Concerning this I entreated the Lord three times that it might depart from me. And He has said to me, "My grace is sufficent for you, for power is perfected in weakness." Most gladly, therefore, I will

rather boast about my weaknesses, that the power of Christ may dwell in me (2 Cor. 12:7-9).

Paul began to look at his handicap from God's point of view. There was a divine purpose behind Paul's affliction. Instead of being a hindrance to his ministry, Paul saw his problem as a "gift" that would motivate him to depend more on God.

All of us face handicaps. They may be physical impairments, sociological disadvantages, emotional disorders, or financial problems. How do you handle your handicap? You have two choices. You can become bitter about it and become utterly useless, or you can choose to look at your handicap from God's point of view.

Does God Want Me Healthy and Wealthy?

I'm a sucker for "success books." In my study I have rows of books written by motivational experts, time-management consultants, and others. When I go into a book store, I make a beeline to the "self-improvement" section. After reading several hundreds of those books, I can boil them down into two sentences: "If you are going to succeed, don't settle for your present situation. Success belongs to those who keep trying." And I believe that is usually good advice.

Some handicaps can be removed, if we are willing to pay the price. Obesity, lack of education, some physical disorders, and financial impoverishment are just some examples of problems that many people have overcome.

The story of Orenthal James Simpson comes to mind. He was born in 1947 in a ghetto section of San Francisco. He suffered from rickets, which stemmed from malnutrition. The rickets caused his bones to soften, resulting in a bowlegged condition. His head also seemed disproportionate to the rest of his body. His mother could not afford costly therapy for her son, so she invented her own therapy. She reversed his shoes, putting his left shoe on his right foot and vice versa. He went through his childhood being called "Pencil-legs" and "Waterhead." Yet, through perseverance, he went on to become one of football's all-time greats! Why? He saw his handicap as a motivation to excel.

But, not all handicaps can be removed by sheer determination. Paul's problem defied willpower. That is why he felt compelled to pray for divine deliverance. Paul begged the Lord on three occasions to remove the problem, but God said no. Don't miss the point. Paul was saying that it is all right to ask God to remove a handicap. But He may or may not choose to remove it.

Contrary to the message of many charismatic preachers, handicaps are *not* beyond the realm of God's will for a believer. In fact, God takes responsibility for all the infirmities that strike people. Remember when Moses was complaining about his speech handicap? He was using his handicap as an excuse for not serving God. "You've asked the wrong guy to go talk to Pharaoh. I'm handicapped!" Moses argued. The Lord's reply is astounding: "Who has made man's mouth? Or who makes him dumb or deaf, or seeing or blind? Is it not I, the Lord?" (Ex. 4:11).

That idea is hard for us to comprehend. God not only allows people to be handicapped—He makes them that way. Why? I find at least three reasons God may allow sickness in a Christian's life.

First, some sickness is given to lead to death. In John 11:4 Jesus spoke of some sickness that leads "unto death." For the believer, death is simply the transition from this life to the eternal state God has prepared for us. And, because of the fallen world we live in, disease and decay ravage our bodies. Yet, this disease is still in God's elective purpose for us since it ultimately leads us into His presence to receive our new bodies. Without sickness we would never die!

Second, some sickness is the result of sin. For example, Numbers 12 records Miriam being stricken with leprosy because of her disobedience. Elisha's servant, Gehazi, was also struck with leprosy because of his greed. In the chapter on David, we saw the physical effects of unconfessed sin as recorded in Psalm 32:3-4. And, today, the disease of AIDS plagues many who refuse to be obedient to God's laws concerning sexual conduct. Sin can be the cause of some handicaps.

Finally, some afflictions are given for the glory of God. It is obvious that it is not God's will for every Christian to be healed. The apostle Paul, who possessed the gift of healing, had to leave his friend, Trophimus, ill in Miletus (2 Tim. 4:20).

One time, Jesus and His disciples passed by a man who had been blind since birth. The disciples, steeped in Jewish tradition, assumed (like many people assume today) that physical impairment was the result of sin. So they asked Jesus if it was this man's sin or the sin of his parents that caused the man's blindness. "Jesus answered, 'It was neither that this man sinned, nor his parents; but it was in order that the works of God might be displayed in him' " (John 9:3).

God allowed this man to be born blind in order that He might be glorified.

In my congregation is a couple whose twenty-three-year-old son is profoundly retarded. They spent years questioning why God had allowed their son to be so severely handicapped.

One night, both the father and the mother were awakened at 2:00 AM and felt impressed to pray for some intervention by God. They were terribly discouraged and were quickly running out of money. But God told them to pray, and they did. The next morning, while waiting to go into the hospital to see their son, a man approached them and said, "I don't mean to offend you, but I want to ask you a personal question. How are your finances holding up?" The wife told the truth, and the man pulled out an envelope filled with hundred dollar bills. He said, "The Lord awakened me at 2:00 AM this morning and told me to give this money to you." It turned out that the man was a multimillionaire; he gave the family his 800 telephone number and added, "If you need any more money, just call me. I am simply a tool of the Holy Spirit, and this is the ministry He has given me."

After relating this story to me, the mother said, "This is the first time in the sixty years of my life that I have ever seen the hand of God." She and her family have a new zeal for God. Because of a financial gain? No, because they have seen the power of God displayed through their son's handicap. I am convinced that God is much more interested in the renewed spiritual commitment of that entire family than He is in the temporary affliction of that son. There is a sickness that God allows for His glory.

It is important to determine if your handicap is removable. Paul's was not. He finally concluded that his handicap was given for the glory of God. Through Paul's weakness, God demonstrated His power.

Making the Most of Your Handicaps

How did Paul learn to live with his affliction? Let me share with you some insights on capitalizing on your handicaps that I find from examining Paul's life.

View Strengths and Weaknesses Realistically

Paul gave a good word of advice to all of us in Romans 12:3: "I say to every man among you not to think more highly of himself than he ought to think; but to think so as to have sound judgment." God has given each of us certain assets and liabilities. A wise person carefully evaluates both. And sometimes that can be painful!

When I was nearing the completion of my theology degree at the seminary, I began wondering whether I should go on and get my doctoral degree. I was tired of school and tried to rationalize not pursuing that advanced degree. One day I had lunch with a Christian leader whose advice I valued. "Look at _____. He's a successful pastor, and he doesn't have a doctorate," I argued. "Yes," my friend said. "But you don't have his looks or his voice. Get the degree!"

Now, that HURT! But, after licking my wounds (and looking in the mirror), I realized he was correct. All of us have certain limitations. But, with those limitations God gives certain gifts, as well.

The context of Paul's admonition in Romans 12:3 is a discussion about spiritual gifts. Paul seems to have been saying that we need to evaluate our weaknesses first, and then we need to concentrate on our gifts.

Define God's Purpose for Your Life

Paul was a man with a vision—God's vision. In Acts 26, Paul recounted his conversion experience while on the road to Damascus. God clearly revealed to Paul his future purpose in life:

> "But arise, and stand on your feet; for this purpose I have appeared to you, to appoint you a minister and a witness not only to the things which you have seen, but also to the things in which I will appear to you; delivering you from the Jewish people and from the Gentiles, to whom I am sending you, to open their eyes so that they may turn from darkness to light and from the dominion of Satan to God, in order that they may receive forgiveness of sins and an inheritance among those who have been sanctified by faith in Me" (vv. 16-18)

Singularly focused on God's purpose for his life, Paul viewed everything else from that perspective. Blessings and hardships both were seen as gifts from God, enabling Paul to fulfill his calling.

For example, Paul found himself in prison at one point in his ministry, awaiting possible execution. "But wait a minute, Lord," he could have argued. "This isn't how it's supposed to work! How am I going to be the world's greatest preacher if I'm stuck here in prison?" Instead, Paul saw this temporary setback as a further opportunity to fulfill his calling.

> Now I want you to know, brethren, that my circumstances have turned out for the greater progress of the gospel, so that my imprisonment in the cause of Christ has become well known throughout the whole praetorian guard and to everyone else, and that most of the brethren, trusting in the Lord because of my imprisonment, have far more courage to speak the word of God without fear (Phil. 1:12-14).

Paul had one, and only one, purpose in life: to spread the gospel. Therefore, his imprisonment wasn't discouraging to him. He was able to see how this "handicap" was helping him fulfill his purpose. First, it gave him a "captive" audience: He was chained to a new guard every eight hours. I wonder what they talked about. Knowing Paul, I'm sure it wasn't the weather, the stock market, or football! Paul said that the "whole praetorian guard" was hearing the gospel as a result of Paul's circumstances. Not only that, but his imprisonment also resulted in other Christians becoming bolder in their witnessing.

The apostle had the same attitude about his physical handicap. God allowed it in order to keep him from becoming proud—an attitude that would have been lethal to his ministry. His handicap also was an opportunity for God to display His power through Paul. Since Paul's calling in life was to proclaim the power of God, he was able to conclude: "Therefore I am well content with weaknesses, with insults, with distresses, with persecutions, with difficulties, for Christ's sake; for when I am weak, then I am strong" (2 Cor. 12:10).

Use Your Handicaps as Opportunities to Improve

As I have said before, there are some handicaps that cannot be removed. But other limitations are really opportunities disguised as problems. A woman had been confined to a wheelchair most of her life. A friend, trying to encourage her, said, "You know, afflictions really color life, don't they?" The woman in the wheelchair answered, "Yes, but I choose the color."[2]

A friend of mine wanted to teach in a seminary. And he is eminently gifted to do so. But when his name came up for discussion among the seminary administration, he was rejected because no one knew him. He was ready to throw in the towel when I suggested that he make himself known. "How do I do that?" he asked. "Why don't you write that article you have been putting off for sometime?" I replied. I mentioned several other projects he had thought of doing but never had the motivation to complete. This present "handicap" was a perfect motivation to improve!

A physical handicap, a job loss, a divorce, or a financial loss may be just the jolt it takes for you to become what God wants you to be! The late comedian Jimmy Durante, known for his long nose, was asked how he dealt with his "handicap" (which, by the way, earned him millions of dollars!). He replied, "All of us have schnozzles!" What is your "schnozzle"? It might just be a great opportunity for you in disguise!

Refuse to Give Up

I'm sure Paul became discouraged about his handicap at times. No doubt he looked at his relentless persecutions and trials and was tempted to throw in the towel. But it was his persistence in the face of adversity that made him successful. He was intoxicated with his goal, and nothing could stop him. "But one thing I do: forgetting what lies behind and reaching forward to what lies ahead, I press on toward the goal for the prize of the upward call of God in Christ Jesus" (Phil. 3:13-14).

The one quality that separates the successful from the mediocre is perseverance—refusing to give up. England's greatest leader, Sir Winston Churchill, was a model of perseverance. At the age of sixty-seven, when other people would be thinking of retiring, Churchill was elected prime minister of Great Britain. With inspiring leadership, he led that nation through the dark days of World War II. In his final days of office, he was invited to give a speech at the public school he attended as a teenager. The headmaster had prepared the boys for weeks, reminding them that they were to hear the world's greatest orator. Finally, the day arrived. After a lengthy introduction by the headmaster, Churchill stood at the podium and gave this brief, but profound, speech: "Young men, never give up. Never give up! Never give up!! Never, never, never, never." And then he sat down!

Perseverance led a tiny nation to victory over the mighty German war machine. And perseverance can make *you* victorious over any handicap.

12
Timothy
Gaining Victory Over Sin's Attractions

"Be careful. Either money or sex will get you." Those were the words of advice I received from my mother, who has now gone home to be with the Lord, shortly after I accepted God's call to the ministry. As a young teenager, I remember thinking how off base she was. Money and sex causing *me* to stumble? Ridiculous! I needed to be on guard against things like doctrinal defection. That's what caused most pastors to fail—I thought. But the passing of time and the revelation about some of God's greatest servants have shown me that my mother was right on target!

My mom's observation was nothing unique. The two letters Paul wrote to the young pastor, Timothy, are sprinkled with warnings to steer clear of the twin traps of money and sex. Just look at some of the references:

> "Fight the good fight, keeping faith and a good conscience, which some have rejected and suffered shipwreck in regard to their faith" (1 Tim. 1:18-19).
> "For the love of money is a root of all sorts of evil, and some by longing for it have wandered away from the faith, and pierced themselves with many a pang. But flee from these things, you man of God" (1 Tim. 6:10-11).
> "Now flee from youthful lusts and pursue righteousness" (2 Tim. 2:22).

Paul knew that if Timothy were to be successful in his ministry, he would have to gain victory over the love of money and the lust of the flesh. You may not be a pastor, but I am convinced that your success in the Christian life hinges on your ability to resist these two temptations. Let's attack them one at a time.

The "Root" Problem

Paul was surrounded by false prophets who thought that godliness was "a means of gain" (1 Tim. 6:5) They preached that being in God's will automatically equaled financial prosperity. Therefore, it naturally followed that *they* should prosper, since they were God's "servants." Isn't it funny how some things never change?

Paul assured Timothy that godliness *was* a means of great gain— but not the kind that the false teachers had in mind. Godliness only profited a person when it was accompanied by contentment. "But godliness actually is a means of great gain, when accompanied by contentment" (1 Tim. 6:6).

What keeps us from being satisfied with what we have? Paul answered the questions in these succeeding verses:

> "Those who want to get rich fall into temptation and a snare and many foolish and harmful desires which plunge men into ruin and destruction. For the love of money is a root of all sorts of evil, and some by longing for it have wandered away from the faith, and pierced themselves with many a pang" (1 Tim. 6:9-10).

The desire to get rich is described as a "snare"—a trap that keeps an animal imprisoned. It causes people to lose their footing and fall into the clutching tentacles of desire. The result is destruction.

Paul said that the root cause of such temptation is a love of money. Now notice that Paul didn't say that money is evil; the love of money is *the* root of all kinds of evil (bitterness is described as a root of evil in Hebrews 12:15). But love of money is *a* source of evil. The love of money caused . . .

the rich young ruler to turn away from Christ,

the rich fool to deceive himself into thinking all was well,

the rich man to neglect Lazarus,

Judas to betray Christ and to commit suicide, and

Ananias and Sapphira to lie to the Holy Spirit and to be struck dead!

That is why Paul urged Timothy to flee from the love of money. How does a person keep from being caught in this trap? The answer, Paul said, is in learning to be content. Let me share with you three keys to contentment.

Key #1: Refuse to Compare Yourself with Other People

The first key to contentment is refusing to play what my friend Howard Hendricks calls "the favorite indoor sport of Christians": comparing ourselves with one another. We love to compare our clothes, our homes, and our bank accounts to those around us. But when we do, we are bound to be discontent. Someone will always have more than you do (unless, of course, you happen to be *the* richest person in the world!).

The Bible calls the game of comparison utter stupidity: "Their trouble is that they were only comparing themselves with each other, and measuring themselves against their own little ideas. What stupidity!" (2 Cor. 10:12, TLB). I learned the truth of that principle several years ago.

As a child I always wanted to be on the "Let's Make a Deal" show. I remember watching Monty Hall and Jay Stewart taunt contestants with the most scintillating prizes. How I longed to have the chance to select Door #1, the box on the trading floor that Carol Merrill stood in front of, or to go for the "Big Deal of the Day." My dream came true on August 4, 1984.

My wife and I were vacationing with some friends in California and heard that the show was looking for some contestants to try out for the next day's episode. We quickly went to the nearest costume shop to select some crazy-looking outfits that would ensure our getting on the program. After all, we were told, the competition would be stiff. We didn't care if we won any money or not—all we wanted to do was to be able to say that we had been on the show. Several hundred dollars later, we drove to the studio (I was in a full-length banana suit. I got plenty of stares on the freeway!).

Much to our surprise, we were selected to be on the show, and it wasn't long into the show until Monty approached me and said, "Robert Jeffress, my next deal is for you!" I ended up winning $350. Then, Monty went to my friends, and they won $1,200.

I'll have to confess that I was envious of my friends. After all, I reasoned, I needed the money more than they did. But what I did not realize was that their prosperity had pushed them into a much higher tax bracket than mine. And they had spent more money on the costumes than I had. So, when all things were considered, we came out about even.

Why is it foolish to compare your life situation to that of another person? Because we do not always know the whole story. The Scripture says that man judges according to the outward appearance. That means we are incapable of knowing the deepest hurts and needs of those we think are "prospering." To desire to be in someone else's position is a foolish request because that desire is based on incomplete information.

Key #2: Trust in the Sovereignty of God

The most important aspects of our lives were predetermined by God: our parents, our heredity, our emotional makeup, along with a thousand other factors. The psalmist declared:

> You made all the delicate, inner parts of my body, and knit them together in my mother's womb. Thank you for making me so wonderfully complex! It is amazing to think about. Your workmanship is marvelous—and how well I know it. You were there while I was being formed in utter seclusion! You saw me before I was born and scheduled each day of my life before I began to breathe. Every day was recorded in your Book! (139:13-15, TLB).

God also takes responsibility for determining our financial destiny. Do you remember Elihu's description of God in Job 34:19? "Who shows no partiality to princes/Nor regards the rich above the poor/For they all are the work of His hands."

I once heard a preacher say, "Each one of us has all the money and power God thinks us capable of handling." That's a sobering thought. Yes, Proverbs is full of insights about how to prosper financially. But ultimately, our financial future (like everything else) is in God's hands. That is the truth behind Paul's words to Timothy in the closing verses of chapter 6. "Instruct those who are rich in this present world not to be conceited or to fix their hope on the uncertainty of riches, but on God, who richly supplies us with all things to enjoy" (1 Tim. 6:17). Get the point? Wealth is nothing to be conceited about because it is God who supplies riches. And He does so according to His eternal purpose.

The truth of the sovereignty of God in every aspect of our lives should not lead us to a fatalistic philosophy, but to a calm assurance from knowing that Someone far more capable than we is in the driver's seat.

Key #3: Develop a Grateful Attitude

The greatest enemy of contentment is expectations. In the back of all of our minds is a certain list of "basic requirements" that we feel God is obligated to meet. And the more we get, the more we expect.

The story is told of a man who went up and down his block passing out ten dollar bills to every household. He did it day after day, week after week, for an entire month. One day, he accidently missed a house, and the owner stuck his head out of the window and yelled, "Hey, where's my ten dollars?"

Paul reminded Timothy of the importance of limited expectations. "For we have brought nothing into the world, so we cannot take anything out of it either. And if we have food and covering, with these we shall be content" (1 Tim. 6:7-8).

Paul was teaching Timothy a crucial key to contentment—gratefulness. Gratefulness is expressing thanks to God for what He has already provided. And, according to Paul, if you have more than food and covering, you are ahead of the game!

Sometimes God may provide more, sometimes less, but the secret to happiness in life is to be content in whatever circumstances you are in.

> "For I have learned to be content in whatever circumstances I am. I know how to get along with humble means, and I also know how to live in prosperity; in any and every circumstance I have learned the secret of being filled and going hungry, both of having abundance and suffering need" (Phil. 4:11-12).

The next time you are tempted to feel discontent about your financial situation, remember these three truths about contentment:

1. God's plan for your life is unique; therefore, refuse to compare yourself with others.

2. God's purpose for your life is based on His elective will; therefore, trust in His sovereignty.

3. God's provisions for your life come from His goodness; therefore, be grateful for what He has already provided.

Paul said to Timothy, and to all of us, that contentment is the secret to gaining victory over the love of money.

Fleeing Youthful Lusts

But what about the second problem, lust? Paul warned Timothy that it was just as treacherous as greed. Paul's pleas to Timothy for moral purity were constant:

> Let no one look down on your youthfulness, but rather in speech, conduct, love, faith and purity, show yourself an example of those who believe (1 Tim. 4:12).
> No soldier in active service entangles himself in the affairs of everyday life, so that he may please the one who enlisted him as a soldier (2 Tim. 2:4).
> Discipline yourself for the purpose of godliness (1 Tim. 4:7).
> Now flee from youthful lusts (2 Tim. 2:22).

"But how do I do that, Paul? I need some specifics!" Timothy must have said. You, too, might feel the need for some practical answers about gaining victory over temptation.

I remember that when I had some questions about sex as a youngster my parents gave me the book *Twixt Twelve and Twenty* by Pat Boone (all I remember about the book were the pictures of Pat and some girls sitting around on a beach in some *very* modest swimsuits). When Timothy asked Paul about this delicate subject, the apostle didn't have a copy of Pat's book to give. But he might have given Timothy another book that was making the rounds at that time. It was by the pastor of the church in Jerusalem. In it are some valuable insights about temptation and how to resist it.

"The Devil Made Me Do It" and Other Myths About Temptation

> Let no one say when he is tempted, "I am being tempted by God"; for God cannot be tempted by evil, and he Himself does not tempt any one. But each one is tempted when he is carried away and enticed by his own lust. Then when lust has conceived, it gives birth to sin; and when sin is accomplished, it brings forth death. Do not be deceived, my beloved brethren (Jas. 1:13-16).

James offered four helpful insights about the subject of temptation.

Temptation Is Inevitable for Every Christian

James began his discussion about this subject with a "promise": Every Christian will experience temptation. Notice that James did not say, if he is tempted but "when he is tempted." James made a distinction between testing (the subject of the first portion of chapter 1) and temptation. Testing always has as its end result the strengthening of a Christian. The phrase "testing of your faith," or *dokimion* in Greek, pictures a piece of pottery being fired in an oven for strengthening. If it does not crack under the intense heat, it is "approved."

In contrast, temptation has as its purpose the destruction of a believer. Notice how Webster defines the verb *tempt:* "To entice to do wrong by promise of pleasure or gain."

Temptation Does Not Come from God

The phrase "when he is tempted" is a present passive participle in Greek that denotes a person who is on the verge of yielding to sin and, right before he or she yields, offers an excuse, "I am being tempted by God." James said that is a lame alibi: "Let no one say when he is tempted, 'I am being tempted by God'; for God cannot be tempted by evil, and He Himself does not tempt any one" (1:13).

Where do temptations originate? James said that we are "carried away" by our inward drive to sin. Not only do our lusts carry us away but also they entice us. The word translated "enticed" is a term used to describe fishing. It could be translated "baited" or "hooked." The word pictures a fish so blinded by its inner craving for food that it fails to see the hook in the bait.

I'm not much of a fisherman, but those skilled in the sport tell me that one of the secrets of fishing is knowing what bait to use on certain fish. Satan is a master fisherman who knows us well. He knows what "bait" to dangle in front of us.

Lust + Opportunity = Sin

James gave a simple equation for sin: "Then when lust has conceived, it gives birth to sin; and when sin is accomplished, it brings forth death" (1:15).

The words "conceived," "gives birth," and "brings forth" all have reference to the birth process. James used this analogy to illustrate that, just as the sperm of the man and the egg of the woman must unite at just the right time for conception to occur, so must lust and opportunity come together to produce sin. When our inward lusts draw us to the outside "bait," the result is sin. And sin brings forth death or *thanatos*—separation from God.

Temptation Can Be Resisted

The liberating truth of the gospel is that we are no longer slaves to sin who have to follow after our inward lusts: "For the power of the life-giving Spirit—and this power is mine through Christ Jesus—has freed me from the vicious circle of sin and death" (Rom. 8:2, TLB).

How can we successfully resist temptation? Do you remember the equation for sin: Lust + Opportunity = Sin? One way we can resist temptation is by removing ourselves from the opportunity or "bait." That was Paul's counsel to Timothy: "Flee from youthful lusts." Paul may have even reminded Timothy of the story of Joseph—another young man who successfully gained victory over sin's attraction.

Joseph was God's man in Egypt. Through a series of miraculous events, he had risen to be head over all of the household of Pharaoh's right-hand man, Potiphar. Potiphar's wife made continual sexual advances toward Joseph. But Joseph held his ground and said to her, "How then could I do this great evil, and sin against God?" (39:9).

Unfortunately, temptation never stops with one refusal. She kept propositioning him "day after day." "Now it happened one day that he went into the house to do his work, and none of the men of the household was there inside. And she caught him by his garment, saying, 'Lie with me!' And he left his garment in her hand and fled, and went outside" (Gen. 39:11-12). Joseph knew himself. Being alone with this beautiful and available woman was more than he could handle. So he fled. He ran so quickly in the opposite direction that Mrs. Potiphar was left holding his coat!

You may be in a situation that can only lead to sin. Like Joseph, you need to run as hard as you can in the other direction.

But sometimes that is not possible. And frankly the "bait" is not the root of the sin problem anyway. The most effective way to resist temptation is by refusing to nurture "lusts." After all, lusts cause us to "bite" at the bait.

How do we refuse to feed our lusts? By controlling our thought lives. By being on guard about the television programs and the reading materials that enter our minds. We may find ourselves engaging in what we believe are harmless fantasies. But after a while these fantasies will turn into lusts. And when they meet the right bait—SIN! It is interesting how something so small as a thought can have catastrophic results.

I remember hearing the story of a man who, driving to work one day, suddenly lost control of his car, landed in a ravine, and died. The investigators ordered an autopsy to try to determine what caused the man to lose control of the car. Was it a heart attack or stroke? But they could find no answer until an observant doctor noticed a small prick behind the man's left ear. Upon further investigation it was determined that a wasp had been trapped inside the car and had stung the man in a very sensitive area of his neck. Blinded with pain, he lost control of the car at a treacherous point in the road and was killed. A small and normally harmless wasp had caused a disastrous result.

It is the same way with our thoughts. Paul told Timothy that if he were to be successful in gaining victory over sin, he would have to "discipline [himself] for the purpose of godliness" (1 Tim. 4:7). Such discipline would have to begin with his thought life. Paul wrote of the importance of "Taking every thought captive to the obedience of Christ" (2 Cor. 10:5). What is the result of a small thought not brought into captivity?

Someone has said:

Sow a thought . . . reap an action;
Sow an action . . . reap a habit;
Sow a habit . . . reap your character;
Sow your character . . . reap your destiny.

13

Priscilla and Aquila
Participating in the Gospel

The most popular image of marriage is one of two people gazing at one another in romantic ecstasy. But, the more biblical image of marriage is that of two people gazing—not at each other—but in the same direction, shouldering the same burden. The most enduring marriages are those built on common goals that can be better accomplished by two persons than by one. No couple better illustrates that truth than Priscilla and Aquilla, the "dynamic duo" of the New Testament.

"Your Tent or Mine?"

This couple is mentioned six times in the Bible (Acts 18:2,18,26; Rom. 16:3; 1 Cor. 16:19; 2 Tim. 4:19). Three of the times the husband, Aquila, is mentioned first. In three other instances, Priscilla is mentioned first. Coincidence? Maybe. But I think Luke and Paul either consciously or subconsciously were showing the true spirit of partnership that existed in this marriage.

As we examine these six references about this couple, we are able to piece together a short biography. Aquila had the family name that meant "eagle." It was the name of a commander of a Roman legion. Nothing is known of Priscilla's background. However, we know that both were Jews who were born in Pontus. They were tentmakers by trade. And so, being an enterprising couple, they left Pontus for the big city of Rome. No doubt, they enjoyed great prosperity in that city until Emperor Claudius banished all Jews from the seat of the Roman Empire.

They decided to take their business to the great commercial city of Corinth. There they met another tentmaker who would forever change their lives:

> After these things he [Paul] left Athens and went to Corinth. And he found a certain Jew named Aquila, native of Pontus, having recently come from Italy with his wife Priscilla, because Claudius had commanded all the Jews to leave Rome. He came to them, and because he was of the same trade, he stayed with them and they were working; for by trade they were tent-makers. And He was reasoning in the synagogue every Sabbath and trying to persuade Jews and Greeks (Acts 18:1-4).

Paul was the first "bivocational" pastor of the New Testament. However, he did not view his having to make tents as a hindrance to his ministry. Instead, his secular vocation gave him a point of identification with his audience. And here is a perfect example. Through Paul's trade, he was introduced to this couple. I am sure that Paul immediately sensed that they were devout Jews but that they were not Christians. Just as Jesus decided to go to Zaccheus's home, Paul decided to go to Aquila and Priscilla's home. Why? There were plenty of hotel rooms in Corinth. But Paul wanted to introduce them to the Savior.

We do not know for sure when this couple was converted. It was obviously sometime during the year and a half that Paul spent in Corinth. When the apostle left Corinth for Ephesus, he had Priscilla and Aquila with him! "And Paul, having remained many days longer, took leave of the brethren and put out to sea for Syria, and with him were Priscilla and Aquila" (Acts 18:18).

Apparently, this couple were not only saved but also immediately gave up their lucrative business in Corinth and devoted themselves to spreading the gospel. Some might suspect that they were just enamored with the apostle Paul. But that was not the case. Even after Paul left Ephesus, Aquila and Priscilla remained, continuing the ministry they had begun.

The single most important contribution to Christianity was their discipling of an Alexandrian Jew named Apollos:

> Now a certain Jew named Apollos, an Alexandrian by birth, an eloquent man, came to Ephesus: and he was mighty in the Scriptures. This man had been instructed in the way of the Lord; and being fervent in spirit, he was speaking and teaching accurately the things concerning Jesus, being acquainted only with the baptism of John; and he began to speak out boldly in the synagogue. But when Priscilla and Aquila

heard him, they took him aside and explained the way of God more accurately (Acts 18:24-26).

When Paul wrote to the church at Corinth, Priscilla and Aquila were still carrying on a vibrant ministry in Ephesus: "The churches of Asia greet you. Aquila and Prisca greet you heartily in the Lord, with the church that is in their house" (1 Cor. 16:19).

No money was available for a church building, so the early Christians met in one another's homes. Apparently this couple was gracious enough to host one of those meetings. That is no small thing. Our church has recently begun a minichurch program to give our members a spiritual boost during the week. Each group is made up of six couples and the meeting rotates from house to house. Although each couple only has to host the meeting twice over a six-month period, I can tell that even *that* is an inconvenience to some. Imagine what it was like for Priscilla to host a much larger group, week after week and year after year.

They kept this ministry up, even after they left Ephesus and went back to Rome. Paul mentioned them again in Romans 16:3-5: "Greet Prisca and Aquila, my fellow workers in Christ Jesus, who for my life risked their own necks, to whom not only do I give thanks, but also all the churches of the Gentiles; also greet the church that is in their house."

They were not only hospitable but also courageous. We do not know what event Paul was referring to here, but it involved putting their lives on the line for the apostle. Maybe it was during one of the Ephesian riots that Aquila and Priscilla saved Paul from being killed by those in opposition to his ministry.

The final mention of this couple is found in 2 Timothy 4:19. Paul was at the end of his ministry, awaiting his execution. As he had opportunity to reflect on his ministry and the "trophies of grace" God had given him, his thoughts turned toward this couple: "Greet Prisca and Aquila, and the household of Onesiphorus."

Ingredients for a Successful Marriage

These few references to Priscilla and Aquila paint a picture of an inseparable couple (you never find one mentioned apart from the other), singularly focused in their life goals. What husband or wife would not enjoy that kind of a relationship with his or her spouse? What factors contributed to their successful marriage?

A Common Heritage

Priscilla and Aquila were from the same side of the tracks. Both were Jews, born in Pontus. They also came from noble families. As I mentioned earlier, Aquila had the family name of a Roman commander. The name "Prisca" was also representative of nobility. Thus, they shared a common background. Is that important in a marriage? Most definitely. Several years ago, Billy Joel recorded the popular song "Uptown Girl." It was a contemporary ballad about love between sociological opposites—a high society girl "slumming" it with a "downtown guy." How romantic! But it has been my experience as a pastor that such marriages are severely handicapped. I'm not saying that differences in background cannot be overcome, but it is far easier if a couple shares a common heritage.

I'll admit that I'm biased. I met my wife when we were both twelve. We went to the same junior high and high school. We lived one street apart from one another and were best friends from the beginning, walking to and from school together every day. The result is that we have the same frame of reference from which to view our present circumstances. We possess a wealth of common experiences from which to draw. And that is an immeasurable advantage in the sometimes difficult task of marital communication. I think that is what the writer of Proverbs may have had in mind when he advised, "Rejoice in the wife of your youth" (5:18). There's much to be said for a common heritage.

A Common Faith

Even more important than their common heritage was their common faith in Jesus Christ. Both Aquila and Priscilla were devout Jews who had come to trust in Christ as their Savior. This faith was the bedrock of their relationship.

Both the Old and New Testaments speak of the importance of a unity of faith. The Israelites were repeatedly commanded not to marry outside the faith (Ex. 34:16; Deut. 7:2-3; Mal. 2:11-12). Paul gave this explicit instruction to Christians:

Do not be bound together with unbelievers; for what partnership have righteousness and lawlessness, or what fellowship has light with darkness? Or what harmony has Christ with Belial, or what has a believer in common with an unbeliever? (2 Cor. 6:14-15).

When a person tells me that he is deeply in love with someone who is not a Christian, I can tell Christianity is not too important for him. Otherwise, how could he be content to live with someone with whom he could not share the most important part of his life?

A Common Purpose in Life

The prophet Amos asked a logical question, "Can two walk together, except they be agreed?" (Amos 3:3, KJV). Imagine getting into a car with your spouse, and asking, "How do we get there?" Your spouse would probably ask, "Well, first tell me where we are going. *Then,* I can tell you how to get there!"

Aquila and Priscilla had their destination clearly in focus. They were going wherever God led them. Their one goal was to be obedient to Him in sharing the gospel with others. That led them to accept Paul's invitation to sail to Ephesus. They were agreed on sponsoring a home church. They must have both consented to risk their lives for the sake of the gospel. And, according to tradition, their mutual faith led them to martyrdom.

A Common Respect for One Another

All right, I'll admit it! I'm reading between the lines here. But I believe I am correct. No marriage could have so successfully endured as Aquila and Priscilla's without a deep mutual admiration and respect for one another.

Being a student of Paul's, Aquilla had probably heard Paul's teachings about the role of women in the church. He was aware of the prohibition against women exercising authority over men in the church. And he and his dedicated wife probably agreed with that. However, they were wise enough not to focus on that one prohibition. Instead, they concentrated on their endless opportunities to share the gospel. They realized that they compensated for one another's limitations. Together they could handle anything.

I think of a story told by commentator Charles Osgood. Two

women lived in a convalescent center. Each woman had suffered a debilatating stroke, one woman's left side being damaged and the other woman's right side restricted. Both had been gifted pianists, but they had given up hope of ever playing again. The director of the nursing home had an idea. She sat them down on the piano bench to play together—one playing the left-hand side, the other playing the right-hand side. They not only made beautiful music together but also formed a beautiful friendship.

That's the message of Priscilla and Aquila's marriage—two individual personalities working together, side by side, in the name of the Lord.

Notes

CHAPTER 1

1. F. B. Meyer, *Abraham* (Fort Washington, Penn.: Christian Literature Crusade, 1983), p. 132.

2. V. Raymond Edman, *The Disciplines of Life* (Wheaton, Ill.: Scripture Press, 1948), p. 54.

CHAPTER 2

1. Charles Colson, *Loving God* (Grand Rapids: Zondervan, 1983), p. 164.

2. Meredith Kline, *The Wycliffe Bible Commentary,* ed. Charles Pfeiffer (Chicago: Moody Press, 1962), p. 463.

3. Joseph Bayley, *The Last Thing We Talk About* (Elgin, Ill.: David C. Cook, 1973), pp. 55-56.

4. C. S. Lewis, *The Problem of Pain* (New York: The Macmillan Company, 1944), pp. 28, 36.

CHAPTER 3

1. Charles Colson, *Loving God* (Grand Rapids: Xondervan, 1983), p. 36.

2. Ibid.

CHAPTER 4

1. Charles R. Swindoll, *Living Above the Level of Mediocrity* (Waco, Tex.: Word, 1987), p. 104.

CHAPTER 10

1. Herbert Lockyer, *All the Women of the Bible* (Grand Rapids: Zondervan, 1967), p. 88.

CHAPTER 12

1. Merrill F. Unger, *Unger's Bible Dictionary* (Chicago: Moody Press, 1957), p. 839.

2. John C. Maxwell, *Be All You Can Be!* (Wheaton, Ill.: Victor Books, 1987), p. 126.